SECOND EDITION

SPORTS JOURNALISM

AN INTRODUCTION TO REPORTING AND WRITING

KATHY STOFER
HASTINGS COLLEGE

JAMES R. SCHAFFER
NEBRASKA WESLEYAN UNIVERSITY

BRIAN A. ROSENTHAL
UNIVERSITY OF NEBRASKA

ROWMAN & LITTLEFIELD
Lanham • Boulder • New York • London

Executive Editor: Elizabeth Swayze
Assistant Editor: Megan Manzano
Senior Marketing Manager: Kim Lyons

Credits and acknowledgments for material borrowed from other sources, and reproduced with permission, appear on the appropriate page within the text.

Published by Rowman & Littlefield
An imprint of The Rowman & Littlefield Publishing Group, Inc.
4501 Forbes Boulevard, Suite 200, Lanham, Maryland 20706
www.rowman.com

6 Tinworth Street, London SE11 5AL, United Kingdom

British Library Cataloguing in Publication Information Available

Library of Congress Cataloging-in-Publication Data

Names: Stofer, Kathryn T., author. | Schaffer, James, 1949– author. | Rosenthal, Brian A., author.
Title: Sports journalism : an introduction to reporting and writing / Kathryn T. Stofer, James R. Schaffer, Brian A. Rosenthal.
Description: Second edition. | Lanham : Rowman & Littlefield, [2019] | Includes bibliographical references and index.
Identifiers: LCCN 2018039888 (print) | LCCN 2018050573 (ebook) | ISBN 9781538117873 (electronic) | ISBN 9781538117859 (cloth : ¬alk. paper) | ISBN 9781538117866 (paperback : alk. paper)
Subjects: LCSH: Sports journalism.
Classification: LCC PN4784.S6 (ebook) | LCC PN4784.S6 S88 2019 (print) | DDC 070.4/49796—dc23
LC record available at https://lccn.loc.gov/2018039888

♾️™ The paper used in this publication meets the minimum requirements of American National Standard for Information Sciences—Permanence of Paper for Printed Library Materials, ANSI/NISO Z39.48-1992.

Printed in the United States of America

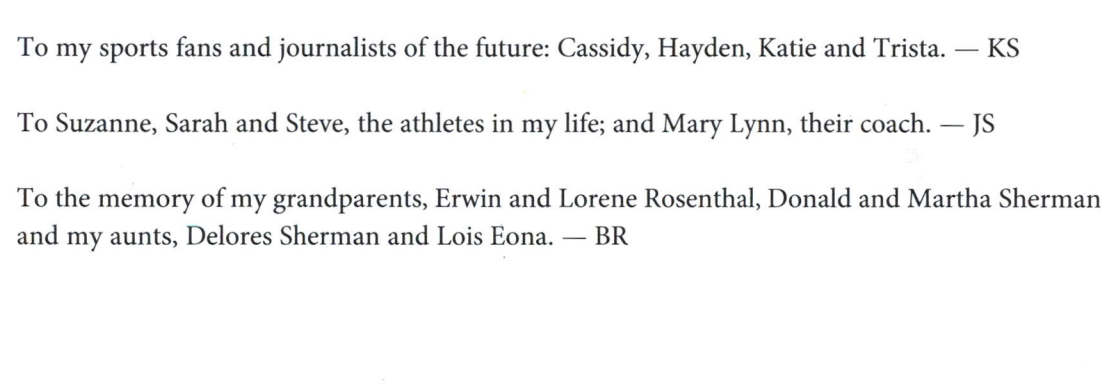

To my sports fans and journalists of the future: Cassidy, Hayden, Katie and Trista. — KS

To Suzanne, Sarah and Steve, the athletes in my life; and Mary Lynn, their coach. — JS

To the memory of my grandparents, Erwin and Lorene Rosenthal, Donald and Martha Sherman; and my aunts, Delores Sherman and Lois Eona. — BR

Contents

Preface

Would you believe that in the decade since the authors first said, "Let's write that book!" fax machines and handheld recorders have disappeared from the media scene, and the cloud has virtually replaced everything once stored on disks and CDs? And that Twitter feed is not something to nourish animals but is the way your news comes to you — at your fingertips — around the clock?

Enter the second edition of *Sports Journalism: An Introduction to Reporting and Writing*. This book has passed the test of time, been used in classrooms internationally and received approval and praise from professors and students, and now it too has moved into the new environment of sports media. New chapters on social media and topical issues in the sports world, as well as fresh examples and new references to current technology, fill its pages whether you choose to read from a tablet, a smartphone, a Chromebook or on old-fashioned paper bound in a cardboard cover.

Sports reporters are journalists who write about sports. They're expected to understand and speak the idiom but write so those who don't can still feel they're in the midst of the action. Fans and editors expect them to know the rules of the game, plus the rules of journalism, and be able to meld the two into colorful, action-packed game stories, picturesque profiles, informative features and thoughtful analyses in as little as 280 characters.

After teaching a course in sports reporting and writing for several years while searching for a textbook that met our requirements, we discovered we were not alone in wishing for a tool that would provide a basic introduction to a sports reporting career and to the writing skills a novice sports reporter or media relations person needs. So we pulled together the curriculum developed for a three-credit-hour course; added examples, suggested activities and discussion topics for further review; and created a book of easy-to-access information. We made the text timely for each class by supplementing it with current examples, trips to sports events and visits with guest speakers.

Inside this new edition you'll find

- Three new chapters devoted to the evolution from a daily news source to a 24/7 news cycle.
- Interviews with journalists whose circulation is measured by the number of Twitter followers they have.
- A chapter encouraging discussion of ethical issues affecting today's athletes: Should college athletes be paid to compete? Can play be too violent? Is there a level playing field for men and women? How should eligibility be determined for athletes who may be transitioning their gender identity?
- A glossary that includes terms such as "hot takes," "scrum" and "trolls."

The authors intend the introductory chapters of "Sports Journalism" to acquaint students with issues and challenges in sports media and the lifestyle of a sports media reporter today, including

- Evolutions in technology.
- The participation of citizen journalists and bloggers who contribute photos and information via media websites and Twitter.
- An industry-wide scaling back on publications, staff and advertising dollars.
- A shrinking news hole created by an industry in transition and a fluctuating economy.
- The need to balance coverage of women's sports and the revenue and nonrevenue collegiate sports with that of professional teams and local school and club sports.
- The erratic hours and deadline-dictated lifestyle of the sports journalist.

The writing skills chapters in "Sports Journalism" elaborate on news values and the conventions of the journalistic genre as they apply to sports writing while providing simple guidelines for novice sports writers. The core of the book focuses on

- Writing in the journalistic genre from news values to nut grafs, inverted pyramids to Model Ts, simple sentences to headlines.
- Using basic writing tools such as S-V-O, active voice and attribution.
- Building relationships with sources, colleagues and media contacts.
- Interviewing.
- Using numbers and statistics.
- Practicing AP style.
- Understanding legal terms that apply to published work.
- Promoting the ethical standards set forth by the American Sports News Editors and the Society of Professional Journalists.

Checklists and illustrations assist writers with such tasks as

- Story organization.
- Sports news releases.
- Media guide content.

Plus there are

- Anecdotes about athletes and sports media writers.
- Glimpses of historical moments in sports journalism.

Upon Further Review at the end of each chapter

- Provides exercises for practicing concepts and skills introduced in the chapter.
- Stimulates discussion of classic and contemporary issues in sports.
- Suggests activities to accompany chapter content.

The back matter adds a practical, professional perspective via

- A sampling from the AP Sports Guidelines and Style.
- The Society of Professional Journalists' Code of Ethics.
- A glossary of sports and media terms.

Assignments that supplement sports reporting and writing classes vary from season to season and school to school, but they usually include

- Writing game stories, features and columns.
- Interviewing athletes, coaches and players.
- Participating in news conferences.
- Exploring print, broadcast and online coverage options.
- Filing stories on deadline from any location.

Every effort has been made to follow the current edition of The Associated Press Stylebook in this volume, as an example to those reading it and preparing to write in that generally accepted journalistic style even when it varies from other style guides and/or dictionaries. AP issues a new edition each year in which it highlights additions and changes. By subscribing to the online version of the AP Stylebook (which includes the AP Sports Guidelines and Style), sports writers will be able to stay up-to-date on style.

Today's sports writer does much more than write about sports. The job description now includes words like blogger, videographer, commentator, talk show anchor and webmaster.

Filled with examples from newspapers, websites, sports books and the authors themselves, "Sports Journalism" is an easy-to-read textbook that can also serve as a handbook to help beginners get started in sports media and media relations careers.

The authors bring a synergistic combination of experience and skills to "Sports Journalism." Among them, they have more than 20 years of professional sports and media writing experience, 50 years of college teaching experience, 12 published textbooks and four graduate degrees in writing and mass communication.

In today's rapidly changing social media environment, the authors recognize that parts of this book are already technologically dated. We also recognize that the fundamentals of writing well and acting honorably and ethically will remain at the heart of the profession, no matter what the medium. For that reason, "Sports Journalism" is dedicated to encouraging those values in journalists who choose to spend their time with the people who play the games.

Acknowledgments

Special thanks to our families, friends and colleagues for their faith, patience, encouragement, belief and many times their willingness to handle extra responsibilities while we wrote this book. It truly takes a team to win the game!

Kathryn T. Stofer appreciates and thanks those who helped make this second edition a reality and who strengthened the text in so many ways: John Wood, Jeanne Tool, Tammie Wall, Pam Bohmfalk, Sharon Brooks and Roger Doerr.

James R. Schaffer would like to thank Joe Gisondi, for reading the manuscript and helping us better understand blogging; Ryly Jane Hambleton, for her many insights into reporting and tireless dedication to her craft; and Karl Skinner, for his encyclopedic knowledge of small-college sports.

Brian A. Rosenthal extends his grateful thanks to Kathy Stofer for allowing her former pupil the opportunity to share what he's learned from the professor and for her friendship and support; to James Schaffer, whose periodic visits over coffee kept a new author from turning gray before he should; to close friend and colleague Mike Babcock for his knowledge, expertise, wisdom and humor, especially during the stressful and trying times of a sports writer's career; to Ted Harbin, Adam Jardy, Austin Meek and David Plati for their professional insight and help in writing this textbook; and to his parents, Eugene and Donna Rosenthal, and sister, Kimberly Hofmann, for their continuing love and support.

1

Living the Life

When I spent more than 20 years writing sports for three different newspapers, including 16 covering Nebraska football and men's and women's basketball at the Lincoln Journal Star, my friends, family and other readers would generally ask me the same questions about my job.

Among them were "Do you get into all of the games for free?" and "Where do you sit?" and, particularly when I covered the Huskers, "Do you get to fly with the team when they play road games?"

The answers, in order, were yes, the press box and no.

However, in my new sports writing position with the University of Nebraska athletic department, the answer to that last question has changed. I do sometimes fly on the team charter for road games. And let me tell you, once you've flown a private charter, going back to commercial flying is a drag.

Yeah, a rough life, huh?

Well, in fact, being a sports writer can be rough, both for a newspaper and an athletic department.

Long hours. Odd hours. Weekend and holiday hours. Hours waiting in an airport parking lot, hoping to eye that potential coaching candidate being whisked away in a Cadillac SUV with tinted windows. Hours counting the few trees along desolate highways in western Kansas.

Hours getting sunburned at state track meets. Hours in the middle of the night when you awake in a cold sweat, wondering if you remembered to put the score of the game in the story you'd written a couple of hours earlier. Hours that eat up your week but never seem to be reflected in your biweekly paycheck.

Hours sharing with friends your most memorable encounters with famous athletes and coaches. Hours laughing about embarrassing moments. Hours in packed stadiums on crisp fall Saturdays. Hours in warm-weather climates in the dead of winter.

Hours remembering you're glad you're a sports writer, after all.

The career field has expanded over the years, too, which is how I landed my new position at the University of Nebraska. The school figures among a handful of NCAA Division I athletic departments (Colorado, Oregon and Wisconsin are others) in that it's hired its own in-house beat writer to cover its athletic teams. The job differs from a regular newspaper beat writer because, obviously, the message will be slanted toward the school and carry a positive tone, whereas newspaper beat writers must remain strictly neutral and cover both the good and the bad, albeit in a fair and balanced manner.

All sports reporters, whether they're affiliated with the school or not, must adhere to one strict rule: There is no cheering at games. Even so much as a fist pounding on a table is asking for, at the very least, a stern verbal warning from a media relations staff member and, at the most, he or she removing you from the press box.

KNOW YOUR TERRITORY

Preparation is the key to sports writing.

For instance, when in El Paso, Texas for the Sun Bowl basketball tournament, I spent some free time in Juarez.

Lee Barfknecht of the Omaha World-Herald and I walked through the streets of Juarez and reached the city square.

A man, speaking through a bullhorn, had a large crowd of more than 5,000 people pretty excited. It turned out he was elected mayor, but he wasn't from the ruling party and he was not going to be seated.

I knew a little Spanish, and Barfknecht asked me what was going on. I said the man was upset. The crowd was agitated and we needed to leave soon, as we were surrounded by policia, some government troops and German shepherds.

We slowly stepped backward, left the city, walked across the bridge to El Paso and stepped into a bar.

A riot had broken out. Water cannons. The dogs going after protesters. Some shootings.

Nebraska played well in the tournament.

— Ken Hambleton, Lincoln Journal Star

ROUTINE? WHAT ROUTINE?

Another common question about my job: "What is your schedule?"

My answer: "What day is it?"

There are no 8-to-5 jobs in sports reporting. That's great during slow times when it might be easy to sneak away on a sunny spring day. It's not so great during state tournaments and coaching searches. And just when you think you're enjoying a Sunday off, a phone call with a tip about a football recruit giving an oral commitment can throw your day out of whack in an instant.

Sports reporting has certainly become more of an "on-call" job. Twitter and social media have turned sports reporting into a 24/7 news cycle. The internet never sleeps. Sometimes, neither do sports writers.

Take this day, for instance. It happened in the middle of my tenure at the Lincoln Journal Star, when I was a secondary beat writer for the football team and the lead beat writer for the men's basketball team.

It's a day I won't forget.

On a cold November morning, the University of Nebraska is expected to fire football coach Bill Callahan. Also that day some 60 miles away, Nebraska's men's basketball team is preparing to play in-state rival Creighton.

Being involved with both events, my day goes like this:

- 6:20 a.m. University athletic department sends out an email, calling for a 9:30 a.m. news conference.
- 6:30 a.m. Arrive on the north side of Memorial Stadium, sitting in my car (heater running) with my coffee cup in my lap and a donut in hand. I notice at least a dozen other reporters. The stakeout begins.
- 6:40 a.m. Step outside my car and make some footprints in the light dusting of snow. Make some small talk with other reporters. We decide it's not likely Callahan or any of his staff members will show their faces here with this much media present.
- 7 a.m. My newspaper colleagues, staked out elsewhere, inform me via cellphone of the "secret entrance" from which Callahan is expected to emerge following his meeting with interim athletic director Tom Osborne.
- 7:20 a.m. Callahan arrives in his Lexus. A security guard opens the gate.
- 7:25 a.m. Osborne arrives in his Chevy Tahoe. He enters the gate.
- 7:35 a.m. Meeting between Osborne and Callahan is over. Callahan leaves and waves to reporters from the windows of his Lexus.
- 7:40-9 a.m. Some furious phone calling, text messaging and typing take place, all to get as many updates as possible on the newspaper's website.
- 9:30 a.m. Attend a news conference at Memorial Stadium, where Osborne announces he's fired Callahan.

- 10 a.m. Gather a few post-news conference quotations from players to assist the main beat writer and columnist in coverage.
- 10:30 a.m. Drive to Omaha for the Nebraska-Creighton basketball game.
- 11:40 a.m. Arrive at Qwest Center Omaha in plenty of time for the 1 p.m. tipoff. Traffic wasn't so bad, what with everyone at home watching the football news conference live on television.
- 1 p.m. Basketball game begins. Creighton takes a commanding first-half lead. I notice Osborne, hours after firing Callahan, is in attendance in a suite. Makes for a good note.
- 5:30 p.m. File story on Nebraska's loss to Creighton.
- 5:45 p.m. Drive through McDonald's. Order the #4.
- 7 p.m. Arrive back in Lincoln at the office. Get up to speed on the latest with football, which is now a coaching search. Make some phone calls to players and offer assistance in other ways.
- 11 p.m. Head home and sprawl out on the sofa.

That's far from a routine day. But in sports reporting, nothing is routine.

A MAN'S BEST FRIEND?

I was at the 1994 Orange Bowl, which started about 8 p.m. and had a halftime that lasted hours, it seemed.

Anyway, Nebraska and Florida State changed the lead four times in the final two minutes or so. I had four 10-inch leads written so I could pop in the score and hit send to beat the deadline for the early edition.

The game ended, our columnist, Mike Babcock, sent my lead, and I headed to the locker rooms for quotes. I sprinted across the field. I didn't notice that police, with police dogs, were surrounding the field.

About halfway to the Husker locker room, a large German shepherd lunged and growled at me. I did a sideways broad jump. Looked back and saw a couple of cops laughing.

I had to keep going. Got my quotes for a better lead story and a sidebar. And after a stop in the Florida State locker room, noticed a bowl of candy in the hallway.

I grabbed a handful, started toward the field to go back to the press box, and threw a handful of candy at the dogs. They went for the candy, and I got to the elevator without the scare.

— Ken Hambleton, Lincoln Journal Star

Whether with the newspaper or the athletic department, for every 16-hour day, there might be a day spent "working" from home. For every recruiting story or coaching search, there's an interview with the next great pro. For every bitterly cold spring junior varsity soccer match, there's a courtside seat at the NCAA Tournament. For every paycheck that you hope lasts until the next, there's a free trip to Los Angeles, Seattle or San Antonio.

And yes, admission is free.

— Brian Rosenthal

TAKEDOWN OR REVERSAL?

Sports writers will find themselves in situations where they need to think quickly and be creative.

For example, I've covered the Kansas state high school wrestling tournament at beautiful Kansas Coliseum in Wichita. The sports writer's challenge, at that time, was one that should not have been a challenge at all: simply gathering results of each match.

The problem was that the Kansas State High School Activities Association, which put an area high school's athletic department in charge of hosting and coordinating the event, was charging media members for typed results of matches. I wasn't the only one who found that practice bizarre, ill-conceived, inconvenient and downright stupid. Who in the world charges sports writers for statistics?

A group of sports writers tried combating the situation by putting one newspaper in charge of obtaining a copy of the official results. The group hauled in a photocopier, had some young volunteers make as many copies as needed, and either handed them out to sports writers or filed them in folders for later use.

It was a fine system . . . until the photocopier croaked (on championship Saturday, no less). Deadlines were fast approaching. Sports writers, having to succumb to the KSHSAA and its member schools' rule for paying for results, were digging through pockets for loose change.

That is, except for one sports writer. He went to the head table, where high school volunteers working for the KSHSAA were forming a line and stapling together final packets of results. Looking young enough to pass for a high school student, he got in line, began piecing together his own packet and went about his business. Nobody seemed to be the wiser.

— Brian Rosenthal

2

Covering the Game

"I always turn to the sports section first. The sports section records people's accomplishments. The front page has nothing but man's failures."

— Chief Justice Earl Warren[1]

On crisp fall Saturdays in Princeton, New Jersey, 10-year-old John McPhee would run onto the field with the Tigers football team and stand on the sidelines with them. McPhee's job was to station himself behind the goalpost after each score and catch the extra point. That seemingly insignificant job, however, led to a life-changing insight:

> One miserable November afternoon, soaked in a freezing rain, I turned around and looked up at the press box. I saw people up there with typewriters, sitting dry under a roof in what I knew to be heated space. In that precise moment, I decided to become a writer.[2]

You may not have had a flash of inspiration quite like that, but if you're smart enough to come in out of the rain, you're ready to be a sports writer.

A NEW KIND OF SPORTS REPORTER

It just might take a little chutzpah these days to be a sports writer. Dave Portnoy, podcast host and founder of a sports blog "Barstool Sports," bragged that he could play a round of golf just as well as the top pros so long as he could have unlimited mulligans. A mulligan is a free shot; in other words, Portnoy, an average golfer at best, could keep hitting the ball over and over and over again until he found a shot he liked.

Sure enough, the ruling authority of professional golf, the USGA, offered Portnoy a chance to play at Shinnecock Hills, the venue for that year's U.S. Open championship. Portnoy could have as many mulligans as he liked, so long as he finished the round in five hours, 15 minutes.

Insane prediction or something achievable? Portnoy ended up with a score of 66 (four under par), estimating that he used about 10 mulligans per shot, or nearly 700 shots for the round! This publicity stunt was great for Portnoy's blog, but it was also a good boost for pro golf after some of the players had complained that the course was just too hard. None of them would want to say now that they couldn't beat Dave Portnoy.[3]

Although Portnoy is a radio broadcaster, his career offers a good clue as to what the next generation of sports writers must be. Most will be mojos, "mobile journalists," who can compose blogs, shoot video and continue to handle all the traditional responsibilities of print journalists.

The New American Sports Fan

Fans have obsessed over their favorite teams, no doubt, for as long as there have been fans, but the internet has helped create a new generation of committed sports fans. Take Will McDonald, for example.

McDonald, a University of Iowa doctoral student, painstakingly records an account of each game played by his favorite team — the Kansas City Royals — on his blog. The blog has become a popular hangout where Royals fans follow the action and swap opinions.

Many post comments such as:

"$3 million a year doesn't get you much these days."

"Never before seen batting order, the 67th of the season."

"Ha Ha Ha!!! I love it! Right off Pujols' dome."[4]

This interest, one shared by thousands of fans across the country, has blurred the line between sports fans and professional journalists. So much so, in fact, that the NCAA escorted a person out of the press box for blogging a live College World Series baseball game. Chris Thorman, who runs the Kansas City Chiefs' blog at www .arrowheadpride.com, said, "It's totally changing the landscape for sports fans. What separates the mainstream media from the typical blogger is the access. The Kansas City Star's beat writer will have more access, will have nuanced conversations with players, and see things we can't."[5]

Today, major sports teams rarely give credentials to bloggers. But that could change. "I think the time is coming when bloggers will be credentialed and at games," said Will Leith, founder of deadspin.com.[6] In what may be a precedent-setting move, the New York Islanders are planning a bloggers' box for an upcoming season — a press-like area set aside just for them.

PHOTO 2.1
Stealing third base is one of baseball's most exciting moments.
iStock Signature/Dmytro Aksonov

In fact, nearly all print journalists are facing the same paradigm shift. According to David Dunkley Gyimah, a pioneering video journalist in the U.K., they must learn to understand "visual narrative" and allow it to drive storytelling.

As Gyimah puts it, "Vloggers [video bloggers] will undoubtedly rule the net. Their short, sometimes idiosyncratic productions are well suited for a medium where time is compressed and users' attention spans shortened."[7]

And that's not all. Increasingly, sports writers are finding it necessary to cover a whole range of stories far outside the normal bounds of playing fields and arenas. They must become pharmacists, for example, to understand the bewildering array of legal and illegal performance-enhancement drugs, such as steroids. They must add the police beat to their repertoire, as a significant number of college and pro athletes run astray of the law.

They must also be prepared to follow their sport into whatever bizarre territory it takes them. On one windy morning, for example, a college rowing team needed rescue after wind-whipped waves started to swamp the boat. The reporter soon found himself at the edge of a lake examining what was left of a racing shell.[8] Joanne Gerstner, a sports reporter for the Detroit News, noted, "Sports writing is really about medicine, business, sociology, psychology. It's a lot more than a home run or a slam dunk. I have to be able to decipher contracts. I have to be able to describe a knee injury."[9]

But just because sports writing has evolved to include new, electronic-based media and a wider field of play does not mean that the essential standards have changed. The age-old principles of good journalism — accuracy and objectivity — still hold.

Irrational Pastimes

Most people acknowledge that the United States is a nation of sports nuts. Sports, too, get nuttier and nuttier. From motorcycle racing on ice to rattlesnake rodeos, each weekend fans turn out for another dubious sport. Battle of the Monster Trucks, anyone? John Cherwa, associate sports editor at the Los Angeles Times, explains:

> Trash sports, that's our official name for them. Because they're not traditional and, in many cases, they're not real. Supposedly, in Atlanta, they have a thing called cat chasing. They throw a cat out of an airplane and then different parachutists try to chase and catch the cat. I don't know if it's true, but I've heard of it.[10]

Not all of these activities actually involve sweating. "Poker players used to be guys avoiding their wives," comments author Michael Lewis. "Now, apparently, they are professional athletes."

And yet sports are one thing that gets Americans fired up. Sure, some Americans like C-SPAN, but their numbers are overwhelmed by ESPN addicts. Occasionally, political leaders can inspire, but none causes grown men to paint their faces, tattoo their chests and howl like werewolves. As Lewis writes, "For every little boy or girl who wants to grow up to be a member of Congress there are, oh, about one million who intend to become major league baseball players or professional basketball players or ice skaters or gymnasts."[11]

For this chapter, we'll turn our focus on the main event: the sports contest itself. We'll skip monster trucks, by the way, and concentrate on more familiar sports. For all the hoopla, color and spectacle, the sports writer's first obligation is to get out to the ballpark — to report, in other words, on the game.

ADVANCE STORIES

The three major game-related sports stories include the advance, the recap (or gamer) and the postgame analysis. Sometimes these stories may be composed days apart, but in the harried life of an electronic sports journalist, they may all be due within a 24-hour cycle. A preview of an upcoming game that compares teams and players, discusses team records and gives lineups is known as an advance. The advance story requires diligence, but the deadline pressure is light.

Athletes will tell you that games are won or lost in practice. Sports writers will tell you the same thing about stories — the key work is doing research before a game. The reporter tries to find out all she can about the teams, the coaches and the issues she will be covering. Sports writer Steve Sipple comments, "Background is the one time when I don't have to worry about asking the right question. It's the one time when I'm able to relax and have fun while I familiarize myself with an athlete or an issue."[12]

SOFTBALL ISN'T BASEBALL WITH CURLS

Softball is not just baseball played with a bigger ball. Tennis isn't outdoor ping-pong. Cross-country is the only sport where the spectators run around the course to watch the race. Volleyball and beach volleyball? Two different sports. Sometimes knowing the subtle differences between sports is crucial to covering them effectively.

Take softball. Obviously, the ball is much larger than a baseball and, as a result, the field dimensions are significantly different. The outfield fences are not as deep since a larger ball does not carry as far, and the bases are 60 feet apart, 30 feet closer than for a baseball field.

The game is also played much more quickly than a typical three-hour major league game. Softball games go seven innings, two fewer than professional baseball, and the game moves at a faster pace. Pitchers do not spend much time worrying about runners who cannot leave a base until the ball leaves their hand. So they just concentrate on batters.

"We don't always rely on the three-run homer like many baseball teams," said Kelley Green, then softball coach at Lock Haven University. "You will have more sacrifice bunts in softball than baseball to move runners into scoring position."

Pitching is also vastly different. In baseball, teams require a rotation of four to five pitchers, who need much more time for recovery. Baseball pitchers rarely go beyond 100 pitches in a single game. In softball, pitchers often pitch on consecutive days, if needed. The underhanded motion does not put as much strain on the shoulders and arms, but the windmill delivery results in pitches that are just as fast.

As with anything, you need to fully understand a sport before you can properly cover it. You can learn much by reading the NCAA's rulebook. You can watch some practices and speak to coaches and players for background information. Obviously, the more you cover games, the more you will learn. (Most of these suggestions are gleaned from Joe Gisondi's blog.)

Prepare, Prepare, Prepare

How can you best prepare to write an advance? First, read all the relevant information you can, from professional magazines such as Sports Illustrated to local sources like your rival school's paper. In so doing you will pick up on how others cover sports and discover possible angles you can use. What happened in last year's game? What's the history between the two schools?

Second, get to know the team's vital statistics. This knowledge will not only give you insights into how the game might play out (i.e., one team often gets off to a fast start) but also give you something to talk about during interviews.

Finally, get to know the people you'll be covering. Go to practices and remain afterward to speak with players, coaches and trainers. Try to establish a good working relationship with them. These people should feel comfortable coming to you with their story ideas. In turn, they should be confident that you will represent their comments fairly and accurately.

It's crucial that you prepare well for interviews with sports figures. Athletes and coaches are often too ready, willing and able to respond to questions with pat answers. How often have you heard a coach say, "It was a really big win for us" or "We are playing the games one at a time"? This information is of little use to you or your readers. You must be prepared to ask as many specific questions as necessary until you get the information you need to write a genuine story, one with something new or insightful. Look for trends. If you're observant, before long you will spot changes, changes you can develop into thoughtful, well-informed questions.

Pregame Tips

Mark Derowitsch, a sports writer for the Lincoln Journal Star, once quipped, "You could train a chimpanzee to write an advance." Indeed, professional sports writers sometimes seem to be monkeying around, because their previews of upcoming games are painfully predictable. The lazy sports writer merely notes the time and place of the game, mixes in a few statistics, and adds a quotation from each coach. This formula produces the same stale story week in and week out.

In this respect, sports writing is similar to news writing. "You're looking for information," explains Michael Wilbon, sports columnist for the Washington Post and cohost of "Pardon the Interruption," a sports talk show on ESPN. "You're looking for documents. You're looking for anecdotes. You're looking for good quotes. You're looking for something the competitor doesn't have."[13]

Your advances, however, shouldn't serve as sedatives for your readers. In fact, they should have exactly the opposite effect. Think about the anticipation your classmates share for the contest ahead. Typically, the next game is the most talked-about topic on campus — among the players, the general student body and even the faculty.

How can you add flavor to your advances? Find an angle that your readers might not know about. For instance, New York Times columnist Selena Roberts devoted an entire column to the pressure women tennis stars feel to conform to certain ideas about body types; she wrote, "Serena Williams, the snippy bloggers have remarked, has been carrying too much junk in the trunk after a winter weight gain."[14]

Each advance you write should include something fresh, something new. Put simply, try to spice up or featurize your advances to keep them from sounding the same. Interviews, historical features or short human interest stories can help create a far more interesting sports page. Of course, don't forget to include the basic information about the game.

The following should be included in each advance you write:

- The significance of the matchup. Will this game decide who goes to the playoffs? Will one team finally win its first game of the year? What are some recent trends?
- Both teams' records, background of the rivalry and last year's score.
- Key players, key statistics, injuries and starting lineups.
- Styles of play.

Don't overlook advances on other sports. The tennis, golf and wrestling teams might not attract the crowds that the football and basketball teams do, but they are putting forth as much effort — and often have as much at stake — as the teams that are more visible. They can also attract large crowds; at Iowa and Oklahoma, wrestling teams fill large arenas for dual meets.

Make sure that the sports activities of both males and females are reported. More women sports writers are entering the field, including Christine Brennan of USA TODAY and Lesley Visser of CBS Sports; their voices will help change the sports landscape. The popularity of the U.S. women's soccer team, for example, is a good sign of just how much readers care, so be sure to cover these events just as diligently as men's sports.

GAME SUMMARY

As a sports writer, you often have the best seat in the house. You might be on press row (usually at courtside), in the press box (high above the crowd) or on the sidelines. Your job depends on your ability to see all of the action with minimal distractions. Your goal is to write the second of the major game-related stories: a game summary or recap of what happened. Part of that job will take you deep inside the game.

Lee Barfknecht, a football and basketball beat writer for the Omaha World-Herald, describes his duties this way:

My job is to take fans where they normally can't go — the sidelines, the field, and the locker rooms. And I have the opportunity to interview the athletes and coaches they don't get a chance to talk to. You have to know how to use the amount of access that you're given.

With access, though, comes responsibility. Fans depend on you to provide insight into the bad news (the cause of the crucial fumble or why the star volleyball player was benched) as well as the good news (a wind-aided home run, perhaps). Most likely, if you're curious about something, your readers will be, too. Almost anything that grabs fans' attention at a game deserves at least a brief description or explanation in your game story.

The key plays may call for more elaboration, too. How, then, should you decide which plays are crucial? The first step is taking detailed game notes that highlight the momentum swings and the key performances. It may seem a bit old-fashioned to "keep the book," but keeping careful notes forces the reporter to pay close attention to the action. For example, look for moments when a basketball team goes on a 10-2 run or when a tennis player wins 12 straight points. Then, see how this fits in the context of the entire game. Prepare to ask pointed questions about those particular moments.

WHOSE SIDELINE ARE YOU ON?

Consider a high school football game where an intense crowd and an overenthusiastic band may have changed the game's outcome. In the closing moments, Fremont High faced a third down and one on their opponent's 7-yard line. The quarterback had to ask the officials to quiet the crowd twice, but when the ball was put in play, one of the Fremont players jumped before the snap, causing a procedure penalty and eventually dooming the drive.

In the Fremont paper, the writer said players had to face "tough odds" on their opponent's home field and left the game with a "sour taste." The Fremont coach was quoted as saying, "Whether it was the noise that caused us to jump, I don't know. It would have been nice if the kids had been able to hear the signals."

On the other hand, the home team's paper credited the win to a "raucous crowd" that "rattled Fremont's effort to overcome a one-point deficit." "The crowd was really enthusiastic," gushed the home team's coach.[15]

PHOTO 2.2
The excitement of the crowd is part of the game story.
iStock Signature/Dmytro Aksonov

When the game ends, a writer on deadline needs to get good quotations quickly. To get these quotes, the writer must ask tough questions — after all, who wants to talk about a loss? In fact, a coach or player may not like many of the questions that he gets, but don't be afraid to do your job. Sometimes you won't get an answer. Sometimes you'll get an angry response. Generally, though, if a question is legitimate, coaches and players will be willing to cooperate.

A Front-Row Seat, but Keep Your Yap Shut

A press pass gets you into the inner sanctum, the holiest of holies — the press box. Usually situated high above the stadium, the press box affords the best seat in the house and munchies galore. Sounds like a fan's dream, right? Wrong. "Sports writers don't root for teams; they root for stories — the more unusual, compelling and head-scratching the better," explains Omaha World-Herald writer Lee Barfknecht.

Sports writers can certainly be emotional in the press box, but it's not the place for shouts of glee or heartrending moans. Working in this venue leaves reporters with only one option: be professional. Cheering for one team or another is a sure way to find yourself getting tossed out of the press box, probably on the widest part of your anatomy. If you cheer, your copy might also be one-dimensional. So, remember: the press box is only for the cheering-impaired.

METAPHORS

"Sports metaphors are everywhere; they permeate all walks of life," says Robert Palmatier, co-author of a dictionary of 1,700 sports metaphors.[16]

"They've always been used because sports are common to all cultures," says Harold Ray, sports historian. "They just make communication easier."[17]

Objectivity?

But a sports writer doesn't have to be completely neutral either. Don't readers expect the local writers to be (secretly, perhaps) rooting for the home team?

Was it the same game? Depends on where you're standing. Sports reporters try to be objective, but they also stress what the players on their team did or didn't do. Writers should avoid taking a hometown angle, unless they're writing a column, and even then they should try to be as even-handed as possible.

Sports Jargon

Good sports writing depends on the same writing and reporting techniques as any other area of the news. But, in addition to following basic style rules, sports writers must also deal with the unique terminology of each sport.

If you've ever been thrown a curve, been driven up the wall or played the field, you can chalk it up to the world of sports.

In baseball, for example, the writer will be expected to use terms such as bullpen, ground-rule double, pitchout, pickle, rundown and sacrifice. In volleyball, fans will expect to see terms such as dink, kill and overhand pass.

On the other hand, beginning sports writers too often rely on jargon and clichés. Jargon is highly specialized language developed for a special use. If you use cagers instead of basketball players or grid mentor instead of football coach, you are using jargon. Your story may be unclear to some of your readers and seem silly to others.

Clichés are trite, overused words or expressions. When you use expressions such as split the uprights or describe a close game as a barn-burner, squeaker or nail-biter, you are merely echoing other worn-out writing. Avoiding clichés will help your stories be fresh and lively.

Postgame Heroics

Dick Enberg, a sports commentator for NBC, once said that "the beauty of all sports is how grown adults can act like little kids." Indeed, sports can bring out the same emotions in 30-year-old professional baseball players as they do in 8-year-old Little Leaguers. Sports writing is about reporting those emotions.

Whether it's a blowout or a close game, every sports event produces at least one prevailing emotion. Capture that emotion in your story. Support it with descriptions and quotations. Make that emotion the theme of your entire story. You'll rarely find a sporting event that doesn't produce some sort of drama you can write about.

How do you evoke that emotion on paper? How do you make the action come alive? In addressing that issue, Daryl Moen, a journalism professor at the University of Missouri, often tells his students the story of a blind newspaper publisher. The publisher would ask reporters to come into his office and tell him about their stories. Often, they would just tell him the facts—the who, what, where, when, how and why of the story. Patiently, the publisher would ask about the emotions that were evident on the faces of the people. He'd leave each reporter with one piece of advice: "Make me see. Make me see your story."[18]

Don't just make your readers see, however. Make them hear the crack of the bat, the rip of the basketball net and the roar of the crowd. Make them smell the locker room after two-a-day practices. Make them feel the volleyball slam against the hardwood floor. Make them taste the bitterness of defeat. In other words, use all your senses — sight, sound, touch, smell and even taste.

PHOTO 2.3
The crack of the bat means everyone's attention focuses on the field of play.
iStock Signature/Peepo

CATCHING A BREAK

Covering the Nebraska State Games has proven to be one of the most interesting things I've done.

One summer I covered the arm wrestling competition.

Two well-muscled guys, both rookies, were first up.

After grunting, straining and pushing for more than three minutes, one guy's arm broke. Snapped. The loud crack. The blood. The bone sticking through the skin.

The injured guy was too shocked to move. The other competitor got sick. Many in the room ran in panic.

I remembered my first aid training and helped the guy until the paramedics arrived. I got a pretty good interview, too. The injured guy said he'd try again next year — left-handed.

— Ken Hambleton, Lincoln Journal Star

For example, Linda Robertson of the Miami Herald wanted to give some scale to the size of pro football players: "Like American houses, Hummers, and hamburgers, football players are a reflection of the bigness of our society."

Paul Solotaroff, writing for Men's Journal, described the incredible saga of star wrestler Kyle Maynard, who has only stumps for arms and legs:

> If you think a limbless teen can't out-point his foes, you've never seen Maynard scamper side to side, darting for a hold. Wrestlers may start matches on their feet, but bouts are won and lost on all fours, and Maynard is already down there, waiting.[19]

But don't overdo it. Make sure you support your descriptions. For example, writing that the volleyball players were "down in the dumps" isn't really honest. Unless you're a volleyball player, you don't know how they feel. Instead, ask the players about their disappointment. Describe their distraught faces and the tears streaming down their cheeks. And then capture the emotion with revealing quotes.

One way to tap all your senses is to draw on specific details to evoke a scene. Take, for example, Rick Reilly's description of how close one golf ball came to dropping into the creek:

> One less drop of rain. One more run of the mower. A cup less of fertilizer last fall. One more breath from a nearby butterfly. A blade of grass with weak knees. An eyelash less luck. Any of these things could have cost Fred Couples the Masters. But somehow, some way, Couples' golf ball hugged the steep slope at Augusta National's 12th hole, clung to it the way a sock clings to a towel fresh out of a hot dryer. The ball steadfastly refused to fall into the water.[20]

If Reilly can make a golf shot, of all things, come alive, just think how dramatic you can make your stories. Effective sports writers use crisp, lively words — especially verbs — to describe the action. Consider this example from Selena Roberts on the presence of several women drivers in the Indy 500:

> Three women earned a place on the starting grid of 33 drivers, a first for a race that cut its teeth in 1911. At 25, Danica Patrick is the commercialized one; at 35, Milka Duno is the mysterious one; and at 26, Sarah Fisher is the experienced one. Never have so many jumpsuits been fitted with curves for ladies who dig the turns.[21]

Covering Professional Events

Imagine you're a college reporter who has covered a few events on campus. Usually you wear jeans and a t-shirt, blending in with the other college students on campus. Suddenly, you receive an unusual assignment: Cover the U.S. Open. You're scared to death. How do you act? What do you wear? As one college sports reporter put it, "I guess my biggest fear is when I go to pick up my media credentials, they'll figure out I'm not a pro yet."

In the case of the country's largest golf event, a writer would probably head for the USGA's Media Center, an aircraft-carrier-size collection of tents. One tent contains the cable-connected desks of 350 journalists who never need to leave the premises to cover the tournament. In fact, they'll probably see more of it if they don't.

That's because their desks face a scoreboard 100 feet wide that presents the hole-by-hole progress of each player. On either side of the scoreboard are two 36-square-foot TV screens where the writers can follow the action as presented by NBC and ESPN.

Does all this work make you hungry? No problem. In one of the tents you'll find a dining area with a dozen TV screens, so you won't miss a minute of the action.

After players finish their rounds, some agree to do a short press conference called a "flash interview," which takes place just outside the locker room. If a golfer has an unusually notable round, he might be invited to a more formal news conference in the Media Center.

But what if you miss a key interview because you're finishing your peanut butter, pickle and olive sandwich? No worries. A stenographer takes notes at each interview, and with breathtaking speed, transcripts of the interviews will have been typed, stapled and placed in wall racks where you can pick them up.[22]

Observe the other professional journalists as they work. In most situations, you'll find journalists swarming around the players after their rounds. Feel free to do the same. You are allowed to record comments made to other journalists, but don't interrupt if a reporter and player are clearly off to the side in a more private setting. You can stand nearby and wait your turn to jump in with some questions. You should try to seek out angles no one else has found. Before the round begins, select two or three golfers to follow — at least for a few holes — so you can get details that won't be visible to the writers in some tent all copying the same comments. Make sure you get out on the course to capture that firsthand flavor.

POSTGAME ANALYSIS

Once the dust has settled and the ink on the game recap has dried, the sports writer has a chance to, as Wordsworth might say, reflect in tranquility, or in other words, analyze what the heck just happened. An analysis is the third kind of standard game article and one that features opportunities for the most writerly kind of prose. Roger Angell, baseball correspondent for the New Yorker, usually files stories months, if not years, after the events they describe took place. He's going for something besides who won and lost:

> When I began writing sports pieces, it was clear to me that the doings of big-league baseball — the daily happenings on the field, the managerial strategies, the celebration of heroes, the medical and financial bulletins, the clubhouse gossip — were so enormously reported that I would have to find some other aspect of the game to study. I decided

> to sit in the stands — for a while at least — and watch the
> baseball from there. I wanted to concentrate not just on the
> events down on the field but on their reception; I wanted
> to pick up the feel of the game as it happened to the people
> around me.[23]

One thing writers go for in analysis pieces is perspective. They seek to compare current performances with those of the past. So Angell, for example, tries to measure one pitcher's great year against others: "Many observers believe that Bob Gibson's 1.12 earned-run average in 1968 is one of the Everests of the game."[24] Comparing a pitcher's achievement to climbing Mount Everest gives vivid testimony to the scale of his accomplishment.

A sports analyst writes for true aficionados, fans who don't need to have every reference explained. Here's Angell on one of baseball's famous moments: "My father told me about the famous last game of the 1912 World Series, in Boston, and seeing Fred Snodgrass drop that fly ball in the tenth inning, when the Red Sox scored twice and beat the Giants."[25]

The game, *that* fly ball. Presumably, the true fan can supply the missing information. The members of baseball's family, Angell tells us, are "devoutly attached to its ancestors and its family records."

Sports writers love adjectives, and an analysis piece is just the right place to use them. Many writers coin inventive hyphenated modifiers such as pennant-winning, ear-wrenching, and one-base-at-a-time attack. They can also indulge their taste for humorous exaggeration. The artificial turf of a football field might have the "consistency of an immense doormat" while a normally gruff manager might turn from a "grizzly bear to Geppetto."

They open the spigot on the full range of punctuation from dashes to italics and parentheses, not to mention the occasional sentence fragment. Sentence structures become exceedingly flexible and free-swinging. Take the following passage, for example, from a description of a Detroit Lions exhibition football game, by George Plimpton. Plimpton was allowed to play quarterback for five snaps, and he steadily moved the team backward toward its own end zone. On his final play, he pitched the ball to a halfback who was tackled on the 1-yard line. After the final play, as Plimpton trudges wearily toward the bench, he notices that the fans start to applaud. At first he can't believe the people in the stands are clapping for him, and then he begins to understand:

> I thought about the applause afterward. Some of it was,
> perhaps, in appreciation of the lunacy of my participation
> and for the fortitude it took to do it; but most of it, even
> if subconscious, I decided was in relief that I had done as

> badly as I had: it verified the assumption that the average fan would have about an amateur blundering into the brutal world of professional football. He would get slaughtered. If by some chance I had uncorked a touchdown pass, there would have been wild acknowledgment — because I heard the groans go up at each successive disaster — but afterward the spectators would have felt uncomfortable. Their concept of things would have been upset. The outsider did not belong, and there was comfort in that being proved.[26]

Plimpton's description probes deeply into the psychology of the game — the certainty fans have, for instance, that what they see players do is impossibly hard. His sentences resemble those of a philosophy professor, except for a delightful metaphor, one where he imagines a popular mayor waving to the crowd from a convertible. Analyzing a game, season or player gives the writer a chance for sheer exuberance. Why not, for example, stretch a metaphor throughout an entire paragraph as Roger Angell does here?

> Steve Garvey always seems to be standing at attention in the batter's box. As he waits for the pitch, his back is straight and his bat shows not a tremor of anxiety or anticipation. His feet are apart, of course, but perfectly parallel with the back line of the box. When he swings, his head snaps down, as if he were checking the shine on his tunic buttons. What he is doing, of course, is watching the ball — really watching the ball. He swings exactly the same way at every pitch: perfect swings. Last year, he batted .304, which is exactly his lifetime average in eleven seasons with the Dodgers. Garvey is a soldier of hitting.[27]

Long before the reader reaches the punchline, he knows he is being carefully set up. The physical description of Garvey, as if he were in a military inspection, the repetition of "perfectly" and "exactly," and the listing of his hitting statistics all suggest a machine-like consistency. Garvey isn't a player; he is a soldier.

Other metaphors are useful when describing the techniques of each game — throwing, catching and hitting, for example — skills that are simple to the point of banality and yet breathtakingly complex (physicists have yet to fully explain how a curveball works). A split-finger fastball, for example, could be described as "baseball's Rubik's Cube"; fielders must deal with "bazooka shots that are lined past them or at them" or cope with a sneaky bunt, "baseball's shiv in the ribs."

Settling back with one of these analyses, the reader feels the arm of a favorite uncle wrap itself around his or her shoulder and senses the joy of yet another trip out to the old ballpark.

UPON FURTHER REVIEW

1. What new challenges do sports journalists face today?
2. Describe the key elements in preparing to write a story about a game.
3. Can a sports writer take sides? Why or why not? What difference does it make if the writer is doing a story or column?

NOTES

1. This quote appears in Sports Illustrated, July 22, 1968.

2. The story of John McPhee's appearance at a Princeton football game is recounted in his article, "Rip Van Golfer," which appeared in the New Yorker on Aug. 6, 2007.

3. www.barstoolsports.com, May 1, 2018.

4. Will McDonald, "Royals Review," www.royalsreview.com.

5. Chris Thorman, www.arrowheadpride.com.

6. Will Leith, www.deadspin.com.

7. David Dunkley Gyimah created viewmagazine.tv to illustrate how one person could create online broadcasts. This quote appears in "insideSolojos: Videojournalism" on his website, www.mrdot.co.uk/videojournalism_today.html.

8. The college rowing team's mishap was recounted by Algis J. Laukaitis in the Lincoln Journal Star, April 16, 2007.

9. This quote appears in "Getting into the game," by Ed Finkel, Medill, Summer 2004.

10. Cherwa is quoted in Funny Times, an American humor newspaper, www.funnytimes.com.

11. The quotes from Lewis appear in his introduction to "The Best American Sports Writing 2006" (Boston: Houghton Mifflin, 2006).

12. Steve Sipple is a sports writer for the Lincoln Journal Star.

13. Michael Wilbon is quoted in "Getting into the game," by Ed Finkel, Medill, Summer 2004.

14. This quote from Roberts' column appeared in the Sept. 1, 2006, issue of the New York Times.

15. These two stories appeared on Oct. 11, 1981, in the Lincoln Journal Star and the Fremont Tribune.

16. Robert Palmatier's book on sports jargon is "Sports Talk: A Dictionary of Sports Metaphors" (New York: Greenwood Press, 1989).

17. Harold Ray is the co-author (with Robert Palmatier) of the "Dictionary of Sports Idioms" (Lincolnwood, IL: National Textbook Company, 1993).

18. Daryl Moen says that "the goal of all writers is to make readers see and smell and feel and taste and hear."

19. Solotaroff's story on Kyle Maynard can be found in "The Best American Sports Writing 2006" (Boston: Houghton Mifflin, 2006), 1-14.

20. Reilly's article on the Masters, "Bank shot," appeared in the April 20, 1992, issue of Sports Illustrated.

21. Roberts' article, "Sports of the times: Creeping equality, a bit of fraternity and a slick of asterisks at Indy," appeared in the May 27, 2007, issue of the New York Times.

22. This account appeared on Joe Gisondi's blog, onsportz.blogspot.com, which has since been phased out and replaced by sportsfieldguide.org. Gisondi has more than 20 years of experience as a sports reporter and now teaches journalism at Eastern Illinois University.

23. Angell's description can be found in the foreword to his first collection of baseball pieces, "The Summer Game" (Lincoln: University of Nebraska Press, 2004).

24. The account of Bob Gibson's exploits appears in "Distance," New Yorker, Sept. 22, 1980.

25. This quote appears in "The Summer Game," 293.

26. This description comes from George Plimpton's book "Paper Lion" (New York: Harper & Row, 1966).

27. Angell's account of Steve Garvey appears in the May 4, 1981, issue of the New Yorker.

3

Navigating the Twitter-verse

The time is 5:30 a.m., you're still asleep, but daylight is breaking, and perhaps you're awakened by the "thud" your Sunday newspaper makes as your neighborhood carrier throws the heavy bundle of newsprint against the screen door of your front porch on a warm summer morning.

Or maybe you were born after 2000 and have zero idea of this phenomenon known as "newspaper delivery."

Truth be told, you probably get your news these days from the internet or, more specifically, social media sites, like Twitter, that link stories to newspapers' websites.

"It's almost like throwing it on somebody's doorstep," said Austin Meek, a sports columnist for the Eugene Register-Guard in Eugene, Oregon. "You give them a link on Twitter, and they wake up in the morning like I do and check their Twitter feed. That's how they find things they're interested in."

Meek, a 2008 graduate of Kansas State University, formerly worked at the Topeka Capital-Journal in Topeka, Kansas. He specifically remembers a member of corporate management one day addressing the Capital-Journal staff about the importance of engaging readers on social media and, specifically, Twitter.

"I just remember people looking around at each other thinking, 'We're never going to use this, what is this stupid thing this person is talking about?'" Meek said.

Today, Meek said he's embarrassed to admit how much time he spends on his phone each morning when he opens Twitter.

"It's a big part of how I gather news, for sure," Meek said. "Most of the things I read, and certainly any breaking news, I usually see it first on Twitter. It's the first thing I look at in the morning, to catch up on whatever happened when I was asleep. The way I consume news, I rarely go to the site where it originates. I usually get to it from a link on Twitter."

Guess what? Meek, as a consumer, represents most of sports fans these days. If they don't subscribe to newspapers or have online subscriptions, they are monitoring news via Twitter and other social media outlets.

RULES FOR TWITTER

To that end, how should sports reporters, both as informers and consumers, handle Twitter, and what rules should they follow?

Here's a general guideline on the do's and don'ts of Twitter usage for today's sports media journalists:

- Do use discretion in what you tweet. No profanity, and as a sports writer, steer clear of politics.
- Do be accurate. You're a journalist. The same rules apply.
- Do engage with your audience. Respond to their questions. Don't simply retweet your favorite accounts and tweets.
- Do try to maintain a positive, lighthearted approach. While not every news item you tweet will be good news, try to keep a positive outlook, in general.
- Do tweet at peak hours. Normally, before 8 a.m., over the noon hour and after 5 p.m. are prominent times to reach sports audiences.
- Do wait until you have a link to a story if you are tweeting breaking news that you know competing outlets do not have.
- Do sometimes invoke good-natured humor, but do not use Twitter as your failed dream of being a stand-up comedian.
- Do not be too snarky. While sarcasm is a common trait of sports reporters, too much of it can turn off your audience. Plus, an overly snarky comment about the team you cover will assuredly find its way back to sources on your beat.
- Do not be too liberal with the block button. As easy as it is to eliminate critics from your Twitter feed, journalists don't want to develop a reputation as being too "thin-skinned." Only consider removing followers if they are overly rude, vulgar or threatening — not if they simply disagree with you. (The "mute" button is a possible alternative).
- Do not say too much and spoil your content. Provide a link to your media outlet's content when you have breaking news, using the content of the tweet as a teaser of sorts.
- Do not overtweet. While there's no steadfast rule on how often to tweet, use common sense in not flooding your followers' feeds.

Hot Takes

In reality, before Twitter existed in the late 2000s, the term "hot take" likely didn't exist in any sports reporter's vernacular.

Today, the term is prominent. Loosely defined, a hot take is a strong opinion likely written for the purpose of promoting a reaction.

Disappointed for Messi but Argentina deserve to go home. Mainly due to Jorge Sampaoli's awful squad selection and poor choices in starting 11 (Agüero and Dybala on the bench?) He should be sacked.[1]

"Paul George actively deciding to spend his prime in OKC as a 5-7 seed is really something."[2]

Is sending hot takes the primary use of Twitter for a sports reporter or columnist? Many would argue it shouldn't be, but the fact remains some sports writers try to garner attention by stating what some would claim are outlandish opinions.

"If that works for you, great," Meek said. "That's not how I have chosen to use it."

Rather, Meek and most sports reporters choose to use Twitter and other social media outlets as a means of engaging with and informing readers.

"I like engaging with people and I like having reasonable exchanges with people," Meek said. "But I'm not really looking to use it to just promote reaction or to get five million people tweeting back at me."

Even though he's a columnist, Meek chooses to not use Twitter as an outlet to post his opinions. If he did that repeatedly, why should readers subscribe to the Register-Guard or visit its website for his actual, complete work?

"If I really have something to say, I'd rather say it in a column where I can actually develop and support it, versus just kind of blobbing it out there on Twitter," Meek said. "If I was putting a lot of hot takes out there on Twitter, I'd probably be getting a lot of that back."

LIVE TWEETING

One of the most popular uses of Twitter among sports reporters is to inform and update followers of a live sporting event, usually a game or news conference. The reasons vary. Some fans enjoy following along while watching the event, either in person or on television, and look for insight from the reporters on a particular play or call. They also want answers to questions they think the reporter may know because he or she is on-site; sometimes the reporter has an immediate answer: "They are wearing throwback uniforms today." Often the reporter must wait to find an answer if the question is more complex.

Other followers, perhaps on the other side of the globe, may use Twitter as their only means to receive live score updates. Or maybe fans are at work during the hastily arranged news conference of a coach's firing and can only glance at their phone now and then for updates of what the athletic director is telling the media.

PHOTO 3.1
iStock Essentials/relif

Here are five tips for live tweeting from events:

1. Tell your audience.

Twitter followers appreciate a heads-up when you'll be live tweeting an event. Send out a tweet at least an hour or so before your game begins. For example, when first arriving at Allen Fieldhouse, take a picture of the arena with a tweet to help set the scene:

This place will be packed 16,300 strong in another 90 minutes when No. 2 Kansas hosts No. 4 Duke in a key non-conference tilt. PG Grayson Allen (sore ankle) is suited and warming up and will likely play, I'm told. Game starts at 7. Follow here for updates.

You've not only promoted the event you'll be live tweeting but you've also informed your followers of some injury information. Other pregame tweets could include who's officiating the game, or television information or series history — any tidbit that helps promote what's about to happen.

2. Use hashtags.

Most events have dedicated hashtags and by using the right one, you will ensure that your tweet is added to the overall conversation. One quick search will typically turn up the event's official hashtag — and it might shed some light on unofficial hashtags that the community is using as well.[3]

For example, the previous Tweet you sent out previewing the Kansas-Duke game could include *#KUBBall* to include or attract Kansas fans, or *#GoDuke* if you're seeking the Duke audience. Some events, especially bigger-profile ones, will have official, neutral hashtags, like *#SuperBowl50* or *#WorldCup*.

Hashtags don't have to wait until the end of your tweet. In many instances, they can simply replace the name of the team in the content of the tweet, thus saving you on your 280-character limit.

3. Provide insight.

While it's acceptable to provide periodic score updates and other statistical information, chances are the majority of your followers either already know the score or are following along with some stat-tracking app that tells them individual point totals or team yardage totals. If you're only tweeting the numbers every five minutes, you're likely to lose your audience.

Don't ignore statistics entirely. Remember, there's the dad stuck in a meeting or in the stands at a midget football game who might be sneaking peeks at his cellphone and depending on you for the score. So, in addition to scoring updates, provide some sort of analysis or information your followers may not know.

> *#Jayhawks seem perplexed early by the #GoDuke surprise zone defense. Kansas down 10-2 at the first media timeout. Looks like Bill Self is making multiple subs in this first break. Allen started and his ankle seems fine thus far.*

4. Engage with your followers.

This is easier to do at some times than at others. That initial tweet you sent to preview the Kansas-Duke game may result in some questions or comments about Allen's ankle. Given the game hasn't started, you should likely have time to reply. Other times, followers aren't replying to original tweets but simply tweeting questions or comments about the game.

Some probably elicit a response. Many others don't. That's up to the reporter's discretion — and time — but make an effort to engage with your followers when possible. You don't want your followers — and, by extension, your readers — to deem you unapproachable.

You can reply directly to the tweet, manually retweet it with your comment or answer at top, or send a private direct message, if needed.

Reporters writing running game stories won't have time to respond to tweets in the final five minutes of the game but may be able to spare some time after the postgame news conference and before writing that final game story. Focus on writing your story, and then maybe take time to engage more on Twitter after your final deadline.

5. Use professional language.

There is a way to abbreviate your words without using unprofessional language. Commonly used acronyms are acceptable, as are abbreviations such as "pro" for professional or "biz" for business. But don't be fooled into thinking a character limit means you can get away with "U" in place of "you" — just don't go there! It's a fine line, but err on the side of professionalism. Remember that every post represents the brand you're cultivating and should maintain the voice you decided upon when creating your social media plan.[4]

Quoting on Twitter

Especially when live tweeting from news conferences, sports reporters will be quoting sources and perhaps attempting to do so directly. As you will learn in chapter 7, a direct quotation is an exact, word-for-word account of what a person says, placed in quotation marks. If you're 100 percent certain you heard every word correctly and in order, as you are tweeting live, then use quotation marks with proper attribution (also see chapter 7).

However, if the person speaking has a longer thought that's pushing your 280-character limit, it may be best to paraphrase what the source says. That means you're summarizing his or her thoughts without quotations, using as many of the same words as possible. It's a safer way of getting the source's message across without the accusation of misquoting under hurried circumstances.

Direct quoting is obviously easier — and sometimes more effective — in a live tweeting situation if the quote is short and easy to remember.

"I guarantee you we will win this game."

And as always, only quote or paraphrase interesting thoughts or newsworthy details from a live news conference. Don't flood Twitter feeds with every single detail from what you're listening to. Pick and choose the highlights.

RELYING ON TWITTER AS A SOURCE

Adam Jardy, a sports reporter for the Columbus Dispatch in Columbus, Ohio, is young enough in the profession to not remember a time where his job didn't require using Twitter.

"If I'm not on it, I'm going to miss out on things," Jardy said. "It provides a lot of information that otherwise it might take me more time to try to find. If I'm dealing with the (recruiting) class of 2020, the team I'm covering is recruiting 40 kids. Well, keeping tabs on those 40 kids without Twitter can be exceedingly challenging."

Via Twitter and other social media outlets, such as Facebook and Instagram, sports reporters have an easier time keeping tabs on recruits — the future athletes who are considering attending the school a beat writer covers. Even current athletes on the college or professional team a writer covers sometimes will deliver tweets that turn into news — sometimes good, other times controversial.

Any beat writer (see chapter 8) covering a college or professional team should follow as many athletes or coaches on his or her team as possible. You never know for certain when a member of the team you're covering will drop breaking news — he's leaving the program, she's injured and having surgery — or deliver some controversial comments that turn into news.

Conversely, those same people you follow on Twitter may announce positive news that could just as easily result in a news story or feature. In any case, following your sources on social media is an easy way to keep tabs on potential news, or a means of contact in case of a need for an interview or information. A click of the button, and you can direct message a source rather than worrying about securing a cellphone number.

When Jardy had the arduous task of covering a coaching search for the Dispatch, during the time Ohio State was hiring a men's basketball coach, he found Twitter a helpful tool. The agent for eventually named coach Chris Holtmann had followed Jardy on Twitter. The agent, mind you, had a history of not being easily accessible to reporters.

"When he started following me, I was like, 'This is good news,'" Jardy said. "I had a line of communication through the process."

Jardy was able to confirm or deny information throughout his coverage of a coaching search through this means of communication with the candidate's agent.

"It definitely makes you more accessible to a lot of different people," Jardy said of Twitter.

Scooping on Twitter

As you will learn in chapter 8, "scooping" the competition means you have reported a sports news story before any members of your competition. That takes dedication, hard work, solid sources and, sometimes, good fortune.

The Lincoln Journal Star, despite having a much smaller staff, scooped competitors when it first reported Nebraska had suddenly accepted the resignation of women's basketball coach Connie Yori. In the era of the 24/7 news cycle, having a scoop for a significant period isn't easy, yet the Journal Star had a 1,600-word exclusive story, confirming through on-record sources that Yori had resigned after an athletic department investigation. It was hours before the larger Omaha World-Herald was able to confirm the story and report it on its website.

For Jardy, the biggest scoop of his career was first reporting the hiring of Holtmann as men's basketball coach at Ohio State. Of course, in 1990, newspapers such as the Dispatch would have breaking news for their print edition in the morning; without the existence of a website to update, competing newspapers had no choice but to wait until the next day to follow with their late story.

"I think about how unbelievably different that would be," Jardy said. "I can't even imagine what that world was like."

Frankly, if you were the reporter on the wrong end of the scoop, the situation was horrifying.

Today, in the 24/7 news cycle, news outlets are lucky to have a scoop for more than 10 minutes before others report the same story — thanks to social media outlets, like Twitter.

"As soon as you break something, it's literally going to be everywhere, like moments later," Jardy said. "There are times where I might have something, but I'm waiting for it to finish publishing on our website before I even tweet it, because there's no point in tweeting something that doesn't have a link. If it's going to be retweeted hundreds of times, you've got to make sure you've got a link in there, too. That certainly impacts how you're choosing to break it."

In reality, the 24/7 news cycle has all but deemphasized the importance of "having it first," although having the story correct is, and always has been, most important.

"If you have it first or you have it second or you have it third, chances are it's all going to be within a very short time frame," Jardy said. "You still have the pride where you want to be first, but it's not like if you're going to get beat, you're going to get beat by an entire day."

There are times where saving an exclusive story — a story competitors do not have — for the newspaper's print edition and then its website can still work. Jardy once wrote a story about an Ohio State basketball player whose mother was murdered when he was a child. The reporter had built a relationship with the athlete and put in a lot of time to where he could bring up the topic and perhaps have the athlete open up for a story.

"He did," Jardy said, "and I had this exclusive story about his upbringing that we held for print. We had a special play, prominent placement. Stories like that, you can hold for print, absolutely.

PHOTO 3.2
Sports fans often follow the game, whether at home or in the stadium, with some sort of electronic device, usually a cellphone or tablet.
iStock Essentials/gpointstudio

"But even then, in those cases, it's, 'Oh, you're running it Thursday? Can we run it Wednesday?' I don't like sitting on things. It's just my general nature. But, if it's something you are confident enough that you think is unique, you can sit on things. You can't sit on breaking news, almost without exception. It's hard for me to envision a scenario where I know Ohio State is hiring its next men's basketball coach and the exclusive will be in Tuesday's paper. That would certainly never happen. But when you're dealing with features and enterprise stories — how much money they spend on recruiting — that type of story isn't going to be broken on social media. There are still times where we specifically plan on having a big print presence and breaking the news, or having the exclusive story that way. Of course, it runs concurrently online."

SATISFYING YOUR TWITTER AUDIENCE

It's important to know your Twitter audience, whether your account has 500 followers or 50,000 followers. Why, primarily, are they following you? What information, analysis or opinion do they seek from you?

As a beat writer for an area college football team that you may know well, it's easy to have a grasp on what your Twitter followers want to read. Football is a mainstream sport. Essential information on Twitter would include recruiting items, score updates and analysis during games, and other breaking news items.

What happens if you are covering a sport with which you are not familiar? Gymnastics? Wrestling? Jardy faced this challenge when he began covering the Columbus Crew soccer team.

"The people who knew me knew I didn't have a soccer background," Jardy said. "In the world of soccer, if you don't have that background, people are generally skeptical of you and why you would cover their soccer team. I dealt with a lot of angry people who just had no belief whatsoever that I would be able to cover the team they cared about. So I got a lot of angry messages from people on Twitter at that time."

Count this as one reason a sports reporter might wish Twitter didn't exist: backlash from followers and "trolls" — Twitter users who simply send negative tweets to garner a reaction from the original person who tweeted.

"It can help. It can hurt. It can be very frustrating," Jardy said of Twitter. "People picking fights with you, or people taking exception to a phrase you might use, then they just stick on that. I remember I had an ongoing argument with a Crew fan because I was talking about the team's depth chart. This guy was like, 'You're a moron, there are no depth charts in soccer, you clearly don't care about this sport.'"

Jardy told the follower to email him, which he did, and eventually the two had a civil conversation over the matter.

"[Twitter] enables me to get to know my audience better, and vice versa," Jardy said. "I feel these days, you can't have a byline and hide behind it. You have to put yourself out there a little bit. I don't mean from a 'I have to be a personality' type of thing, but I can use Twitter to occasionally post things about my kids, or 'I just bought this album.' I feel those kinds of things show your readers who you are, and they kind of get to know you a little bit."

Twitter is part of the 24/7 news cycle. Long gone are the days of sports reporters writing one game story and heading home or to the nearest pub. No longer do sports reporters attend a news conference at 10 a.m., go home to mow the lawn in the afternoon, take a nap and come back to write the news conference story to beat the 10 p.m. print deadline.

"I think about my game day experience these days," Jardy said, "where I've already written something for the morning, and I've written a pregame blog post, and I've been on Twitter all day and I get to the arena, so I'm getting all my pregame stuff done and getting ready to file my running gamer.

"Then as soon as my game is over, I'm going to interviews, then updating the game story (with quotations), plus write a sidebar, plus a postgame blog, and then there's something that will usually come out of it that I'm trying to write for the next day. You're talking about, for one game, seven or eight different pieces of content."

TWITTER IN THE CLUTCH

Sometimes sports reporters must quickly shift gears and use their reporting skills for breaking events that are not at all sports-related.

Thanks to Twitter, Adam Jardy was able to produce and update a news story for his newspaper, the Columbus Dispatch in Columbus, Ohio.

Serving then as the beat writer for the Columbus Crew, a professional team in Major League Soccer, Jardy was covering a home game when a fierce thunderstorm developed. Not only did the severe weather delay the game, it created a news story.

"We all saw the bolt of lightning from the press box, and the game was delayed for obvious reasons," Jardy said, "and then I saw somebody tweeted me and said there was a man struck by lightning."

Jardy's first course of action was to ask the public relations staff of the Columbus Crew, although they were not able to confirm.

"But then they got a message in their headset, and this guy goes running out of the press box, so I grab my umbrella and I go running, too," Jardy said. "There are like seven or eight ambulances on their way to the parking lot. I head out there, and I cover the thing from the scene."

Indeed, lightning had struck a man in the stadium parking lot. The man was an off-duty fireman.

Jardy did what any good reporter would do. He interviewed witnesses, talked to police officers and firefighters on hand and carefully looked over the scene. He was able to gather various bits of information and write a breaking news story for the Dispatch website.

"Then I'm walking around the stadium, and I find the coach, and he has some more information," Jardy said. "They end up postponing the game, because it's very touch-and-go whether this person is going to pull through or not."

Jardy was in the press box, rewriting his story with new information, when he received another tweet from a reader. He then followed the person on Twitter, "and it happened to be one of the paramedics that was literally in the ambulance with the person who had been struck by lightning."

The paramedic contacted Jardy because he wanted to clarify a medical term Jardy had incorrectly used. Jardy was thankful the paramedic was not only cordial and understanding but also able to provide more information.

"So he helped me out with that, but then they were also giving me updates," Jardy said. "'Yes, he's alive, yes, he's conscious; we're going to the hospital.' I got a sizable amount of information that made my story from direct messaging with an EMT who was in the ambulance with this person.

"That never would have happened without Twitter."

— Brian Rosenthal

During the search for the men's basketball coach that eventually ended with the hiring of Holtmann, Jardy constantly updated his Twitter feed and the Dispatch website every day, three to four times a day. The more a beat writer calls and texts and digs, the more often he or she will have the latest information to update readers.

"We wanted to have the newest information on our website to drive people there," Jardy said. "I might learn that an assistant coach had interviewed for the job and nobody else knew that. That was like a midday update on our Ohio State coaching search. That morning, it might have been, 'These are the candidates they have expressed interest.' Then 2 o'clock, they've interviewed one of the assistants, and by the evening, they still don't have a coach, so you're just summarizing, and by nighttime, it was everything that had happened that day for print the next day: What have we learned since the last time we printed a newspaper?

"For that week when they were searching for a coach, I probably updated my main story to the web three or four times a day."

MESSAGE BOARDS: SOURCE OR NOT?

Some sports reporters might deny they ever visit fan message boards. Fans of college or professional teams can visit a certain website, usually recruiting-related, and express their thoughts and opinions, converse with other fans — or fans of the opponent — and do it all under the nice, tidy anonymity of a goofy name like "Bobcatbob327" or "Weluvthedawgs!"

Even high school coaches and athletes are not immune to the crazed fan who praises, criticizes or spreads gossip — sometimes true, most times not — under an anonymous screen name.

Time used to be when such rumors highlighted visits to coffee shops or the local barber. Regardless the locale or format, the rumors begin, then grow and then somehow gain credibility with some fans or perhaps innocent bystanders who know no better. The problem, of course, is that nobody is held accountable, whether the information is accurate or simply a hoax. Hence, many sports reporters will say they would rather deal with a migraine on deadline or chew tinfoil than associate themselves with message boards.

However, those beat reporters who say they ignore message boards entirely are probably fibbing. If they are really telling the truth, they should probably face reality and admit that, like it or not, anonymous message board posters — sometime referred to as citizen journalists — are part of their job.

For example, perhaps Bobcatbob327, a regular on his favorite fan message board, posts something he has heard about his team — the Bobcats, of course — and the prized freshman quarterback who is deciding to transfer because he is unhappy with playing time. The rumor spreads quickly. You, the beat reporter (see chapter 7), receive a text message from your friend, who has read this hot item on a message board. The rumor has probably made the rounds on Twitter, too.

Can you afford to ignore this tip simply because it appeared somewhere anonymously? Probably not. Do you immediately write a story using the message board as a source? Definitely not. But as with any anonymous tip, you, the beat writer, begin digging, asking, checking and verifying.

Bobcatbob327 might be right, and even though some of his message board buddies will praise him for the scoop, other fans will wait until you, a responsible beat reporter who is held accountable, verifies and reports the news.

What if your late night, last-minute digging is all for naught, and Bobcatbob327 turns out to be wrong? Well, this is a good time to remind yourself of one of the perks of being a beat writer, and you can look forward to a bowl game trip to San Diego. In other words, this is just a normal headache beat writers must handle.

Ideally, beat reporters would have such information about freshmen quarterbacks before it finds the fingertips of a rapidly typing anonymous message board regular. But let's face reality: In a 24/7 news cycle, even the most astute and responsible beat writer can't possibly know of every little detail before cyberspace does.

These are not necessarily everyday occurrences for beat reporters. But a thorough beat reporter will at least keep tabs on some message boards, whether for possible tips or just to gauge the pulse or feeling of the fan base. Some topical feature stories could result, too.

None of this, however, means beat reporters should depend solely on message boards for information. Nor does it mean beat reporters need to or should interact on message boards, anonymous or not.

TWITTER FOR MEDIA RELATIONS

Ted Harbin, owner and editor of Rodeo Media Relations, said social media has become the go-to medium to help promote anything that needs it. He utilizes his news and information website, TwisTedRodeo.com, as a hyperlink to share the stories that he produces for clients on social media platforms.

In addition, anyone involved in promotion must understand the keys to reaching people via social media while also maintaining the appropriate budgets, Harbin said.

One aspect of what Rodeo Media Relations does is focused on social media marketing. Whether it's creating memes or sharing stories, photos and videos, the goal is to get a message to as many viewers as possible.

In event promotion, the primary purpose is to sell tickets to that event, to entice potential buyers that the rodeo performances are worth their money. "It's not just about the posts, though; It also is about the reach and boosting that reach as well as possible. I share my posts with as many of the appropriate people as I can," Harbin said.

Each client has specific needs, though. For some rodeos, it's beyond putting butts in seats. They want to be recognized nationally. Each year, 20 rodeos from across the country are recognized as the very best — five events in four size categories: large outdoor, large indoor, medium and small.

"To obtain those honors, votes are tabulated by the card-carrying members of the Professional Rodeo Cowboys Association, most of whom are the contestants," Harbin said. "To that end, my job is to reach out to as many voters as possible on behalf of those clients. Social media is the best way to do that."

For media relations departments at athletic departments of major colleges and universities, the proper use of social media is emphasized to student-athletes, particularly to those of higher-profile sports.

The University of Colorado media relations department has a handbook for coaches and student-athletes, and also speaks to student-athletes about what to tweet and — more importantly — what not to tweet.

"The underlying theme we tell them in person is, 'If you're tweeting something your mother wouldn't want to see, you probably shouldn't tweet it,'" said David Plati, associate athletic director with sports information at the University of Colorado. "It's kind of like taking your photo. Does your mother really want to see your photo with that frown on your face? When in doubt, you refer to what Mom wants, and it's usually quite effective."

Even a tweet that exists for a mere seven seconds before being deleted, if it's controversial in any way, shape or form, will still likely be nabbed on a screenshot and exist for eternity. Specifically, political, sexist and rude comments, or unflattering comments about the upcoming opponent, could result in punishment for student-athletes.

UPON FURTHER REVIEW

1. Log on to Twitter and follow 10 national sports writers or columnists, and also follow 10 local sports writers or columnists responsible for a particular team or sport. How do their tweets compare and contrast? What type of insight do they provide?
2. Create a Twitter account and attend a news conference or live sporting event and provide updates using appropriate hashtags specific to that audience. See how many more followers you have by day's end, and interact with a couple of them.
3. Follow 10 professional athletes over a month's time, or longer. Compare and contrast their content, paying particular attention to any potential newsworthy items.

NOTES

1. Tweet from Joseph Mechling, @JMechling_36, June 30, 2018.

2. Tweet from Dan Wolken, @DanWolken, June 30, 2018.

3. Laura Dugan, "10 Tips for Tweeting During Live Events," July 11, 2015, https://www.adweek.com/digital/10-tips-for-tweeting-during-live-events/.

4. "Ten Tips to Up Your Twitter Game," undated, http://blog.stickyalbums.com/10-tips-to-up-your-twitter-game.

4

Choosing the Words

Every sport has rules, and every player knows the penalties. Break an NCAA rule and your team may have to forfeit a game. Make too many fouls, and you will be out of the game. Step out of bounds and the play ends.

Sports writing has rules, too: grammar rules, spelling rules, punctuation rules.

You may not be thrown out of the game for breaking a writing rule, but there is a penalty. With each mistake, you lose credibility with your audience and your employer. Make too many mistakes that someone else has to fix or that get into the media, and you will lose your job.

Not only are there rules to learn, there's a sports idiom to master. The sports idiom is a language spoken by insiders and somewhat familiar to followers. It's a combination of sports terminology, slang and cliché that has grown up within the world of sports over the last century or more and has become sportspeak in broadcast, particularly play-by-play. The idiom is so pervasive that some of it has leaked into everyday conversation. Calling something par for the course comes from golf, to strike out or touch base comes from baseball and how about that photo finish that horse racing chipped in? You make a pit stop, spin your wheels or win by a nose. Or you might be thrown a curve, driven up the wall or find yourself behind the eight ball.

Professional writers take language rules very seriously because they know their audiences and their editors respect good writing. Bloggers, emailers, tweeters, scriptwriters, news release writers, sports writers and columnists who use correct grammar and spelling in everything they write will be regarded as professionals by everyone who reads their work.

In addition to knowing and using grammar rules, sports writers are challenged by the complexity of their audiences. Sports fans range from the novice to the know-it-all. The sports writer must craft stories informative and entertaining enough for the novice to enjoy and complete, accurate and technical enough to hold the attention of the die-hard sports fan.

WRITING IN NEWS STYLE

Sports reporters are journalists who specialize in writing and broadcasting about sports and the people who participate in them. Sports stories are based on facts and verifiable information and are written in journalistic style.

Look carefully at the structure of sports stories online, in the newspaper and in sports magazines. In general, a journalistic-style story will have

- Facts and information.
- Short, subject-verb-object sentences.
- Short paragraphs.
- Short words with precise meanings.
- Action verbs.
- Quotations with attribution.
- Numbers and statistics.

And it will not have

- Misspelled words.
- Grammatical errors.
- Misplaced modifiers.
- Weasel words.
- Clichés.
- Euphemisms.
- Redundant phrases.
- Gender-biased language or -isms.

Facts and Information

Sports stories are based on facts, information and quotations. Information is gathered from sources or observed by the reporter. If the information is used in the form of a quotation or paraphrase, it is attributed to the source. Quotations may contain the source's opinion, if the source is identified.

Stories do not include the reporter's opinion. Opinion is reserved for columns and should be clearly labeled as such. In print or online, a column is identified by the writer's column head and byline. In broadcast, opinion segments are introduced as opinion and often delivered by the author in a neutral setting so viewers have audio and visual cues by which to identify opinion as different from game coverage or sports news.

The difference between a fact and an opinion can be as simple as a few words.

Fact: The game went two extra innings during which the Cubs changed pitchers three times.

Opinion: The game went two extra innings because the Cubs' manager made three questionable pitching changes.

Facts are verifiable. Opinions are often expressed in sweeping generalizations laden with superlatives: most famous, best ever, greatest play.

Fact: Nick Saban has coached six teams to the college football national championship.

Opinion: Nick Saban is the most famous coach in college football history.

Blogging, Twitter and Instagram have opened other venues for expressing opinions, both of the sports journalist and of the participating public. Newspapers and television stations have multimedia websites on which they invite people to participate in the community conversation about issues and ideas via social media, written entries, photos and video.

Verify Information

"If in doubt, leave it out."

Phil Andrews, "Sports Journalism"[1]

The first goal for journalists is to be accurate. Journalists never assume anything. They always verify information before putting it in a story. Verification is checking information by comparing it to information from reliable sources. A generally accepted guideline is to check information with three unrelated sources. If three sources agree, it's probably correct and safe to use the information. Note the word "probably" in the last sentence. If there's any doubt in your mind or you have a gut feeling that something is not quite right, don't use it until you're satisfied that it is correct.

The best way to gather facts and information is to attend the event, observe the activity and the people and take notes or record the action yourself. What you observe may be reported without attribution, but verifying statistics and spelling ensures the accuracy of your story. After the event, verify your notes using data and stats sheets from the sports information office, the news conference with the coaches and your own interviews.

If you cannot attend the event, contact the sports information director ahead of time to get players' names and numbers and background on both teams. Make arrangements with the coaches or media relations director for phone interviews after the game and ask for game stats to be faxed or uploaded as soon as they are available.

Short, S-V-O Sentences

Short sentences make text easier to read according to readability tests. Standard readability, or a level easily understood by most media readers, contains about 17 words per sentence.

Not every sentence will be 17 words. Using a variety of sentence lengths creates writing that is more interesting to read.

Subject-verb-object is the preferred sentence organization pattern in journalistic writing. It's easy to read and understand. It makes the subject do the action, and it helps the reader move through the story quickly and easily. S-V-O sentences pack in enough of the who, what, where, when, why and how for readers to have an overview of the story in one sentence. Stringing together all that information tends to make lead sentences longer than the average.

This lead from the USA Today Sports Weekly, for instance, uses 38 words — more than twice the length of the average sentence — to include almost all the information:

> Patriots wide receiver Troy Brown [who] spent time playing defensive back [did what] over the last three seasons [when], and it prepared him [why] to make the critical fourth-quarter play [what] that helped turn an apparent Chargers victory into a 24-21 Patriots comeback win [how].[2]

Daily publications usually break leads into shorter, punchier S-V-O sentences. These five Ws and an H leads from wire services tell the whole story.

> AUSTIN, Texas — Texas' [where] Destinee Hooker, the two-time defending NCAA high jump champion [who], will skip track [what] this season [when] to train with the U.S. women's national volleyball team [why] before the Olympics.[3]

> SALT LAKE CITY — Tag Elliott [who] of Thatcher, Utah, was in critical condition one day after surgery [what] to repair extensive facial injuries sustained in a collision with a bull [why].
>
> Elliott, 19, was riding a 1,500-pound bull named Werewolf on Tuesday [when] in the Days of '47 Rodeo [where] when their heads smacked together [how].[4]

S-V-O is the preferred sentence order in broadcast as well, because it creates easy-to-say units of thought that the listener can understand and absorb while the sportscaster is speaking. Online readers read in chunks: a blurb, a lead or a paragraph. They, too, are looking for easy-to-read, easy-to-understand information, and that's what S-V-O sentences deliver.

Short Paragraphs

Look at the two columns below. Of the two, which would you choose to read first? Why?

At first glance, most readers would choose the column on the right. It just looks easier to read. The short paragraphs, multiple entry points and added white space within the story give the impression that it's a quick read.

In journalistic style, one and two sentence paragraphs are the norm. Newspaper and online stories appear in narrow vertical columns with only a few words on each line, making even short sentences fill three or more lines.

Few programs have garnered as much attention in NAIA athletics as the Hastings College women's basketball team. And there's good reason. Under the direction of head coach Tony Hobson, the Broncos have become a perennial power — riding the heels of three national championships in six years.

The team captured its first NAIA Division II national championship on March 12, 2012, with a 73-69 come-from-behind win over Cornerstone, Michigan. It was the first team championship in school history.

The Broncos, who found themselves trailing by as many as 12 points in the game, rallied behind the play of All-American selections Sophie Taylor, Katie Jade and Cassidy Wall. The team finished that season 34-3 overall.

But the Broncos weren't finished with the national spotlight. One year later, on March 18, 2013, the team became just the second team in NAIA history to win back-to-back women's national basketball titles.

Few programs have garnered as much attention in NAIA athletics as the Hastings College women's basketball team.

And there's good reason.

Under the direction of head coach Tony Hobson, the Broncos have become a perennial power — riding the heels of three national championships in six years.

The team captured its first NAIA Division II national championship on March 12, 2012, with a 73-69 come-from-behind win over Cornerstone, Michigan.

It was the first team championship in school history.

The Broncos, who found themselves trailing by as many as 12 points in the game, rallied behind the play of All-American selections Sophie Taylor, Katie Jade and Cassidy Wall.

The team finished that season 34-3 overall.

But the Broncos weren't finished with the national spotlight.

One year later, on March 18, 2013, the team became just the second team in NAIA history to win back-to-back women's national basketball titles.

TELEVISION SCRIPT

Scripts for 10 p.m. (04-07-2017)

SO8 CASTING CONTEST   Sun. 10 p.m.

PKG
00:00:28

Talent
Hayden Rob

OTS
147
Sports Generic

JUST ABOUT EVERYTHING IS A COMPETITION THESE DAYS.

LIKE RUNNING ON LOGS IN THE WATER . . . OR RACING TURTLES.

VO

Locater — Ticker
Casting Contest
Tooele (two-WILL-uh)

HERE'S AN INTERESTING ONE FOR YOU . . . A FISHING-POLE CAST-ING COMPETITION.

IT'S SIMILAR TO DARTS.

THE COMPETITORS AIM FOR A TARGET AND ARE AWARDED POINTS FOR ACCURACY.

16 KIDS TOOK PART IN TODAY'S STATE FINALS AT THE BOAT DOCK IN TOOELE (two-WILL-uh).

12-YEAR-OLD TRISTA MAIRIN (MARE-en) OF KEARNEY (CAR-knee) WON TODAY'S EVENT.

AND SHE'S HEADED TO NATIONALS IN LAS VEGAS.

#

Paragraph indentations create small white notches along the left margin that make stories appear easier to read by giving readers frequent entry points. When set in columns, longer paragraphs give the impression of black pillars holding up the headline. Readers tend to skip the longer paragraphs because they are perceived to be more difficult to read.

WRITING FOR BROADCAST

Broadcast journalists speak in a conversational tone, but don't be fooled by the ease with which they speak. Conversational does not mean incorrect. Television and radio stories are written with the same care, precision and attention to language as print and online stories. If anything, broadcast is more difficult to write because stories are shorter and each word has to pack so much power.

Spelling and grammar are important in scripts because someone is going to be reading them while speaking the words on air. A misspelled word or incorrect subject-verb agreement can make the reader hesitate or stumble.

Pronouncers, phonetic spellings enclosed in parentheses, are inserted in scripts beside names or words that might be unfamiliar to the speaker. Include a pronouncer with any name or word that can be pronounced more than one way, or is not pronounced with the commonly expected inflections, in a script prepared for someone else to read. It might keep the new sports anchor from pronouncing Cairo as (kEYE-row) when the residents of the town by that name in your market say (CARE-o).

Broadcast writers use single-sentence paragraphs and short sentences, or just a series of short phrases connected by ellipses, to assist the person who will be reading the story on air. Indented entry points help the television sportscaster deliver the story while appearing not to be reading from a script or prompter. The white spaces separate sentences and make it easier to move from one to the next without searching a black block of text to find the next one.

Script format style for television or radio will vary from station to station. Most are divided into columns with the technical cues on the left and the text on the right. Some prepare scripts in the traditional ALL CAPS format. Others use the sentence-style capital and lowercase letters. Some double-space copy; some triple-space copy.

If you're writing for specific stations, know and use their preferred styles.

JARGON: ON THE AIR

Actuality   recorded excerpt inserted in audio news story

Lead-in   short phrase or sentence that sets listeners up for the story

Incue   first four words of a sound bite or actuality, written into the
                script; helps identify correct sound bite

Outcue   last four words of actuality or sound bite, written into script,
                cue to newscaster to begin speaking

Sound bite   recorded excerpt inserted in an audio or video news story

OTS   over the shoulder; picture or graphic seen behind television
                announcer

Tag   lines of the announcer's script that close (end) the story

SOT   sound on tape

Still frame   a fixed photo image taken from a video recording

Still store   an electronic memory unit for storing single screens

VOSAT   voice sound over videotape

SFX   sound effects

EVERY WORD COUNTS

Newspaper editor Stanley Walker, a proponent of the new, the fresh, the descriptive phrase, thought sports writing had reached new heights during the 1920s and 1930s, as young, college-educated writers joined the ranks of veterans like Charles Dryden, Ring Lardner, Damon Runyon and Grantland Rice. Walker summed up the dilemma a sports writer faces in his 1934 book "City Editor":

> The subject matter of sports is pretty much the same. Almost every murder, suicide, shipwreck and train collision is cut on a different pattern, and the reporter does not have to seek outlandish substitutes for common terms. One baseball game, however, is pretty much the same as any other. The few standard verbs and nouns used in writing of baseball, football and boxing become tiresome.[5]

Short, simple words are easier for a reader scanning a story or someone listening to a broadcast story to comprehend. And they take up less space on a page or screen and less time on air. When there's a choice, choose the shortest, simplest word that does not diminish the meaning of the more difficult word.

Replace technical terms and long words with shorter ones.

abrasions and contusions	=	cuts and bruises
torn meniscus	=	knee injury
muscle degeneration	=	muscle damage

Action Verbs

Close your eyes and picture eight-time Wimbledon tennis champion Roger Federer ambling out onto the court to return a 145-mph serve by 11-time French Open winner and opponent Rafael Nadal. Next slide: soccer great David Beckham dancing toward the goal. Next slide: Triple Crown winner Justify stands quietly at the gate, head bowed in the rain, waiting for the race to begin.

Writing that uses descriptive nouns and action verbs helps readers and listeners visualize. When the verb implies an action not indicated by the rest of the image, it interrupts the reader's expectation and makes the listener pause. It's like the sound of screeching brakes in heavy traffic. It draws attention to itself and away from the flow of the story.

Tennis players don't amble when responding to a serve. They sprint, stretch, bound, leap and swing. Soccer players don't dance when moving the ball toward the goal. They may race, run, kick or score, but they leave dancing to the ballroom. Horses nervous for a race to begin snort, rear, stomp, strain — almost anything but stand quietly.

Live coverage and video allow viewers to understand the action by seeing it for themselves. Readers expect to feel as though they are seeing the action when they read about a sporting event. Readers rely on the writer's choice of verbs to help them see how the player moved and feel the difference between a stroll, a strut and a sprint. They want to sense what it's like to dive for a ball, to feel the texture of the bat in their hands, to watch the ball approach and hear it connect, to run the bases and slide in to score.

Attributive Verbs

An exception to the action verb guideline is attribution. When someone is quoted in a story, quotation marks indicate that the person spoke those exact words. The name of the speaker is linked to the quotation, along with a verb of attribution. "Said" is the appropriate attributive verb to use when identifying the speaker. Any other verb carries a shade of meaning that the writer has put on the speaker's words, giving the reader an impression that may not be what the speaker intended. "Shouted," "growled," "stated," "assured," "blurted," "mentioned," "commented," and other words that describe vocal inflections connote meaning beyond the words being said.

Each of these attributive verbs gives a different meaning to the coach's words:

"You are always an injury or two away from being pretty average," the coach explained.

"You are always an injury or two away from being pretty average," the coach sighed.

"You are always an injury or two away from being pretty average," the coach growled.

Words that describe facial expression describe action: smile, grimace, scowl, wince, wink, frown. Words are not actions, and they cannot be smiled, cried or growled. Let the reader decide from the content of the quotation and context of the story how the speaker might have sounded saying the words. If it is necessary to indicate both speaking and facial expression, use both.

Correct: "That play worked well for us," Coach Boeve said.

Correct: "That play worked well for us," Coach Hobson said with a smile.

Avoid: "That play worked well for us," Coach Creech bragged as he grinned.

Misspelled Words and Usage Errors

"A misspelled name is second only to an incorrect score, the two most obvious—and unnecessary—errors."

— Steve Wilstein[6]

Spell check and grammar check are your friends. Visit them often. But remember that, like people, they're not always perfect. Spell check will not identify a correctly spelled but misused word, even if it makes no sense in the sentence. It won't change *no* to *on*, *how* to *who*, or *tea* to *tee* or *team*.

Unfortunately for journalists, spell check does not work on names. The only certain way to know how to spell someone's name is to ask that person.

Grammar check may identify what it suspects are incorrect uses of a word, but the writer must decide which is the correct word. Homonyms such as "there," "they're" and "their" sound alike but are spelled differently and have unrelated meanings. If you have trouble remembering which is which, create a memory trick to help remember the meaning of each word.

When *heirs* inherit money, it is t-*heirs* and *they'(a)re* rich!

They can go here and t-*here* as long as t-*heir* money lasts.

Now it's easy to tell if "there," "their" or "they're" is used correctly in a sentence. Are these?

"Our players are not going to have targets on *they're* backs this season. *Their* physically and mentally prepared to win."

"We're a little weak in pitching. *There's* no experience *their* this year."

"*There* the best players in the line-up."

Correct usage would be:

"Our players are not going to have targets on *their* backs this season. *They're* physically and mentally prepared to win."

"We're a little weak in pitching. *There's* no experience *there* this year."

"*They're* the best players in the line-up."

Collective Nouns

Collective nouns describe more than one person, place or thing as a unit: class, committee, team, group. A collective noun may represent all those individuals as a single unit, or it may represent those single units as individuals. "Team" is the collective noun most often used in sports.

A team, whether it has two members or 200 members, is one team and requires a singular verb or pronoun when referred to as a whole: *The team is leaving Friday.* If the members of the team are acting individually, "team" uses a plural verb or pronoun: *The team are expected to work out for an hour each day, sometime between noon and 6 p.m., and log their times on this form.* For clarity, use "team members" or "players": *Team members are in the weight room working out. The players are warming up.*

The same principle applies to the names of teams. If referred to by the name of the university or the home city, a team is one unit and uses a singular verb or pronoun:

The University of Arkansas *is* favored by 17-21 points.

Miami won *its* season opener.

PHOTO 4.1
Fans cheering on their team don't care if the Longhorns are favored or the University of Texas is the favorite. They are only interested in whether their team wins!
iStock Essentials/monkeybusinessimages

If the team is referred to by mascot or name, it represents the individuals and uses a plural verb or pronoun:

The Razorbacks *are* favored by 17-21 points.

The Dolphins won *their* season opener.

Misplaced Modifiers

Modifiers should be placed as close as possible to the words they modify. If they aren't, they often distort the meaning of the sentence. At best, the result is confusing; at worst, sadly comical. Dangling participle is a fancy name given to modifying phrases beginning with an "-ing" verb bumping up against the wrong noun or pronoun. For example:

Having summarized the main points of the story in the lead, the reader should then be provided with the details in order of their importance.

Did the reader summarize the main points of the story, or did the writer do that? The subject who performed the action should immediately follow the introductory phrase. This sentence could be corrected to read:

Having summarized the main points of the story in the lead, the writer should then provide the reader with details in order of their importance.

In sports writing, dangling participles make images like these:

Trailing 14-0, the burden fell on Troy Aikman.

Studying sports writing last fall, my academic performance dropped.

Running down the field, his shoe flew off.

Or headlines like:

Complaints about NBA officials growing ugly

Aging expert joins coaching staff

Weasel Words

fun	a lot	numerous
some	various	a little
very	few	good (as in "it was a good game")
great	many	different

Some words — even short, simple ones — just don't say anything. What is "fun"? An athlete might say "winning." A fan might say "watching my team win." But if a fan said, "Fun is seats on the 50-yard line at the Rose Bowl on a 66-degree New Year's Day watching my team complete the winning touchdown after the clock runs out!" the audience understands "fun."

Weasel words waste space and don't move the story ahead. If each word in the story does not add, through its specific, concise definition, to the visual image the writer is trying to create, it is a weasel word. Replace it with a definitive word or example:

A lot: 16 tons
90,000 fans
1,122 pennies
5,280 feet
all the blades of grass on a soccer field

Few: the holes-in-one I've made in my lifetime
the members of my bowling team
the number of blind climbers who have reached the top of Mount Everest

Great: winning an Olympic gold medal
holding a winning lottery ticket
achieving a personal best

Quotes that don't add information to the story are just bigger weasel words. If a source says, "It was a great game," ask what made it great. Ask the source to define "great" in that context or to compare this game to another "great" game. A little more time spent asking for specific details means less time spent trying to write a story that shares something worth knowing with the audience.

Clichés

Down for the count, throw in the towel, snatched victory from the jaws of defeat . . . well, you get the idea, old clichés are dead as doornails.

"If you've heard it or read it 10 times, it's a cliché. Don't use it!" is the mantra of many an experienced writer. Clichés are other people's expressions, often described as trite and overused, repeated by speakers and writers but understood, literally or historically, by few. Recognize any of these?

put the final nail in the coffin	always gives 110 percent
draw first blood	a nail biter
hit it through the uprights	turn the tide of the game
sat down with (interview)	gut-check time
off to the races	get that monkey off his back
all over but the shouting	records are made to be broken
go out and leave it all on the ice	always come through in the clutch

The more a cliché is used, the less power it has to engage people's imaginations. The goal is to write the expression that becomes the new cliché (oops, sorry, that's an oxymoron), or to put a new twist on one as this headline does:

Third Tynes a Charm for Giants

Even two-word combinations become clichéd if people recognize them.

> Alexandre Vinokourov and Andreas Kloeden, Team Astana's top two title contenders, were injured in nasty spills Thursday in the thrilling and bumpy stage through the Burgundy winemaking region.[8]

The names of the cyclists and the fact that they are the top two title contenders can be verified. That they took "nasty spills" is the clichéd opinion of the writer and says little to the reader about the falls or the condition of the men or their injuries. The

CLICHÉ SPEAK

Sometimes as writers we have our backs against the wall. We have editors who expect our A-game every time we metaphorically lace up the cleats. That's when I revert to what has been working: clichés.

But you can't win them all. Your editor would have a field day with your work, and your readers would think you've gone to the well once too often.

Unfortunately, there are days like this. But what can you do? Sports are all about winning, and clichés are a proven winner.

Who hasn't ever drained the buzzer beater shot to clinch the win in OT? Who hasn't wanted to punch one across the goal line for six?

And who else but the media can add onto the excitement with such bland, overused terms?

Don't get me wrong. Scored, made, missed, run — they all tell what happened, but they hardly take your writing to the next level.

Some of us are wily veterans of the sports writing world and don't have to try the "Hail Mary" when we're down and out.

But we freshmen phenoms want to dive into the playbook for something fantastic.

We try to describe the things that don't show up in the stat column. We try to bottle up the emotion and capture the moment in words.

Covering sports is a team effort and I'm happy making my contribution, but there has been a lot of trash-talking out there.

Some bad words between writers have caused some extracurricular activity to take place on the field. I tip my hat to them. They made a point that clichés can be boring and useless.

I don't want to point fingers. I only have to look in the mirror to see who is to blame. I couldn't get it done in the clutch, and I shied away from the pressure.

You just have to put the past behind you. My old arm isn't what it used to be.

I hope I can become a living legend, go out on top. But you know, you win some, you lose some, and a tie is like kissing your sister.

So the moral of the story? Throw those old clichés out of your news stories.

And if you're keeping score at home: 34 clichés.

— Isaiah May[7]

JARGON: ON THE PAGE

Flag	name of the paper or website as it appears on the first page
Headline	summary of story content, above story
Subhead/ secondary head	second headline, also called a deck
Byline	reporter's name, run with a story
Dateline	the place, and historically the date, a story happened
Cutline/caption	words describing a picture
Photo credit	source or photographer's name run with a picture
Copy	body of story as written
Rule	lines used to separate elements on a page
Jump	continuation of a story to another page
Slug	label given to a story in progress
Double-truck	spread that covers two facing pages, including gutter
Gutter	narrow strip of white space between columns of text; especially center of double-truck
Pagination	assembling page layouts electronically
Morgue	place archived issues are stored, may be newspapers, film, tapes or electronic files

section of the route through Burgundy can be comparatively bumpy or smooth, but that it is "thrilling" is also the opinion of the writer. It may be scary to one person, challenging to another, and yes, "thrilling" to some.

Euphemisms

A sports writer is like the reporter who was assigned to write a feature about bananas. He thought readers would tire of reading "banana . . . banana . . . banana," so he substituted "that elongated yellow fruit." The sports writer, too, searches for new ways to write about the same old things and ends up with a euphemism instead.

The sports page is the birthplace of many euphemisms. Little has changed since editor Stanley Walker wrote "the few standard nouns and verbs . . . become tiresome." Thus did a left-handed pitcher become a "southpaw," although, Walker observes, "For some reason, right-handed pitchers never were 'north-paws.'" A pitcher's throwing arm was his "salary wing," and "a baseball became 'the old apple.'"

A euphemism is a word substitute used to make something sound better, nicer, fresher or just different. It's a way of sugar-coating reality, making it taste better or sound more exciting. Euphemisms are created when sports writers are trying to find a new, lively, colorful way to say the same old thing.

football	=	pigskin
goal posts	=	uprights
basket	=	hoop
football field	=	gridiron
wrestlers	=	grapplers
cross-country runners	=	harriers

Using a euphemism to replace an accurate action verb is the equivalent of using attributive verbs other than "said." The euphemism substitutes a verb that is subject to interpretation by each person who sees or hears it.

In most sports, for example, players run. If the ball carrier ran, he ran. He didn't plow, gallop, break loose or trot, because he's a human being, not a horse. If she made the shot, she scored. She didn't drain, sink, nail, knock down, swish or put two on the board.

Euphemisms for "run" or "ran" permeate the sports idiom. Use them sparingly. Here are just a few euphemisms for "run":

rambled	rumbled
rattled	broke loose
plowed	bounced off
skipped	danced
flew	galloped

Redundant Words and Phrases

Redundant phrases say the same thing twice or attempt to qualify a word that, by definition, stands alone. Take the commonly used "all-time record," which is a way of trying to make a record sound more important than, by definition, it already is. The record is the highest, fastest, most or best for as long as data have been kept on that activity or event. "Set a new record" is also redundant, because only one record exists at a time.

An old record is no longer a record. It is now second place. Hank Aaron held the most-home-runs-hit in Major League Baseball record at 755 for more than 33 years. But as soon as Barry Bonds hit his 756th home run, that became the record. The number hit by Aaron will forever be Aaron's best, but it is no longer the record for number of home runs hit by one player.

Redundant terms like these often appear in sports contexts:

a team of 12 players	ultimate outcome
close proximity	new record
completely outplayed	new recruits
end result	true facts
favored to win	totally destroyed
free passes	future draft choice

Even the football staple "sacked the quarterback" is redundant. The quarterback is the only position that can be sacked. It pays to study the terminology for the sport you're covering.

The Language of -isms: Sexism, Racism, Ageism

Forget you ever heard the cliché "throw like a girl." It's kid stuff compared to the -isms some broadcast personalities have been using on the air.

Nationally syndicated radio talk show host Don Imus was fired in April 2007 for using a racial slur in reference to members of the Rutgers University women's basketball team. It took a week and a public outcry to make his employer, CBS Radio, take action against Imus.

Imus had violated one of the -isms: sexism, racism, ageism. And the listening audience was outraged.

The -isms have changed the language significantly in the last half century. Historically, the white male has been assumed superior in U.S. society and in its written documents. "We hold these truths to be self-evident, that all men are created equal." Two constitutional amendments and more than two centuries later, women and minorities are still struggling against sexism and racism to achieve equal treatment. Sports, where female and minority athletes have long excelled and been recognized for their achievements, may be the exception. Or maybe not. In many U.S. cities, in California, and in the world as a whole today, whites are the minority.

But be careful of the alternatives. Don't describe people by what they're not. If non-white covers all persons of color, are whites non-colored? Is a redhead non-blond? Is a

PHOTO 4.2
Editors gather for a budget meeting before each news cycle, confident that their writers are skilled grammarians familiar with AP and news style.
iStock Essentials/G-stockstudio

shortstop a non-pitcher? The authors of "When Words Collide" suggest writing sensitively and accurately about people in any collective such as age, race or gender; think of people in terms of individuals, not as representatives of, or exceptions to, a group.[9]

Generally, ageist language reinforces stereotypes by expressing surprise over those who do not conform to them. The focus of this story implies that the accomplishments of NFL quarterback Brett Favre, who led the Green Bay Packers to victory in Super Bowl XXXI, are "sensational," an anomaly for someone past "his prime":

> DETROIT — Brett Favre was asked to throw 17 straight passes at one point. The way he was completing them, the Green Bay Packers didn't need to hand the ball off.
>
> Favre set a franchise record with 20 consecutive completions and finished with a season-high 381 yards and three touchdowns in the Packers' 37-26 Thanksgiving Day victory over the slumping Detroit Lions.

"You never think he is going to miss one," Green Bay coach Mike McCarthy said.

The three-time MVP put together another sensational performance that made the 38-year-old Favre look as if he's back in his prime. His seventh 300-yard game of the season matched a team mark he set 12 years ago.

— Larry Lage, Associated Press[10]

Straightforward, factual writing devoid of descriptive adjectives, stereotypical allusions or labels that indicate a person is a member of a specific gender, race or age group is the best way to eliminate accusations of -ism bias in writing.

Oh, yes. Imus was back on the air before the end of the year.

7 STEPS TO ERROR-FREE STORIES

- Double check rosters, numbers and statistics with officials at the game.
- Run spell check, grammar check.
- Read for content and structure.
- Read again to edit words, spelling, punctuation.
- Read the story aloud.
- Ask someone else to read the story.
- Read the story from end to beginning.

PROOFREADING

"Accuracy, accuracy, accuracy" was Joseph Pulitzer's admonition to reporters and copy editors when he was the editor of the New York World in the 1880s.

He might have added that a simple way to achieve accuracy is to proofread, proofread, proofread.

Proofreading begins with the writer, who should correct errors before filing a story. Some errors only you will recognize because you're the one who asked the sources to spell their names or saw the coach put an arm around the shoulders of a player who was having a bad day. Which player was it — number 23 or number 32? Was the player's name Cheri, Shari or Sherry?

STRATEGIES FOR ACHIEVING ERROR-FREE STORIES

1. Use spell check and grammar check. Even if there's no time to do any other editing, take advantage of these helps built into your software. Even an eagle-eyed copy editor will never be as fast at finding and fixing errors as these electronic checkers.

   But look carefully at the suggested corrections before making a change. The computer-generated correction may change the content in such a way that the message is no longer what you intended.

   Spell check won't flag a correctly spelled word, but you will know if the word is "would" when it should be "wood" or "king" when it should be "kind."

2. Read the story from beginning to end just to get a sense of what it says. Do not stop to make corrections.

   The goal at this stage is to analyze the story: Does it have all the necessary information? Does it flow easily — that is, will readers be able to follow the story and understand what they've read? Are quotations in appropriate places to explain points you were trying to make? Is it organized appropriately for the content? Does it need a conclusion, or does it have a conclusion but need a wrap to the lead?

   This is the time to add information, reorganize paragraphs or insert a quote.

3. Print the story and read it again, this time penciling in corrections in sentence structure or punctuation, changing words that are misspelled or don't seem quite right for the context.

   This is where you'll catch errors spell check didn't. Only the writer will recognize a misspelled name or know if the game was Friday or Saturday or whether the score is reversed.

4. Read the story aloud. You may see mistakes because your eyes have to look at each word long enough for your brain to get the message and send it to your vocal cords. You may hear mistakes in sentence structure or find sentences that need to be shortened. If a sentence is too long to read aloud without taking a breath, it's too long.

   The author of "AP Sportswriting," Steve Wilstein, calls this the mumble method. "I read sentences and stories aloud to myself, kind of mumbling along the way, so that only I can hear what it's about and whether it makes any sense. By mumbling just loud enough, I can pick up the sound of sentences and the connections between them and better spot errors."[11]

5. Read the story to someone. Better yet, have someone read it to you. If the reader stumbles over a word, hesitates or stops midsentence, those places are going to be a problem for others, too.

6. Read the story aloud backward. Start with the last word and read from right to left, enunciating each word. This is the ultimate test to make your eyes focus on each word. In reading from left to right, readers see phrases or groups of words and may not realize one word is repeated or missing, or that there's an "s" on the end of a word that should be singular. By forcing your eyes to look at each word, you are more apt to recognize an error.

UPON FURTHER REVIEW

1. The sports idiom is a language unto itself used by insiders and fans with total understanding. Make a list of 10 words and phrases you found in today's sports news that you think are a necessary part of the idiom and 10 words and phrases that you think are meaningless clichés and euphemisms. Share your lists with the class and discuss where you think a reporter should draw the line in a game story. Is it the same for play-by-play? game analysis? columns?

2. Find three sports stories in which euphemisms or clichés are used. Highlight the euphemisms and clichés. Revise the stories, replacing the euphemisms and clichés with more accurate, precise language.

3. As language evolves, usage changes. In some contexts, including media, the plural possessive pronoun "their" is becoming acceptable with a singular noun or pronoun antecedent. Example: A player should work on their skills in the off-season. Read sports stories from several sources, paying particular attention to sentences containing "their." Is the antecedent in each use singular or plural? How important do you think it is for writers to adhere to the rules of grammar? Why? Is it acceptable to use "their" in media writing as a substitute for the gender-specific "his" or "her"? Why or why not?

NOTES

1. Phil Andrews, "Sports Journalism" (London: Sage Publications, 2005), 74.

2. Jim Corbett, "Chargers get lesson in playoff pressure," USA Today Sports Weekly, Jan. 17-23, 2007, 15.

3. "Texas' NCAA high jump champ to skip track season for volleyball," www.usatoday.com/sports/college/2008-01-22-texas-hooker-volleyball_N.htm?csp=34 (accessed Jan. 23, 2008).

4. "Bull rider critical with head injury," Dallas Morning News, July 27, 2007, 2.

5. Stanley Walker, "City Editor" (New York: Frederick A. Stokes Company, 1934), 119.

6. Steve Wilstein, "Associated Press Sports Writing Handbook" (New York: McGraw-Hill, 2002), 112.

7. Isaiah May, "Cliché Speak," Hastings College Class of 2009, Norfolk, Nebraska.

8. Jerome Pugmire, "Vinokourov, Kloeden crash in Tour de France," Associated Press, Hastings (Nebraska) Tribune, July 13, 2007, 3C.

9. Lauren Kessler and Duncan McDonald, "When Words Collide" (Boston: Thomson Wadsworth, 2008), 182.

10. Larry Lage, "Favre leads Packers past Lions," Associated Press, Hastings (Nebraska) Tribune, Nov. 23, 2007, 1B.

11. Wilstein, "Associated Press Sports Writing Handbook," 182.

Writing the Story

One Man's Mission

At a glance, Richmond Country Club, just north of Oakland and directly across the bay from San Francisco, appears no different than most other private clubs in the United States. There is a sturdily built stucco-and-brick two-story clubhouse, in the Tudor style; rich green, kempt grounds; a quiet, unhurried air.

In the men's locker room, however, there are photographs on the walls indicating that in this place a bit of golf history was made. They are pictures of Sam Snead, Toney Penna, George Schoux and E.J. "Dutch" Harrison when they won the Richmond Open, a tournament played from 1945 through 1948 as part of the pro tour's winter West Coast swing.

Then again, if a picture that was never taken also dressed the wall, it would peg the club as the site where a considerably more significant historical event took place than the likes of a Sam Snead winning a golf tournament. It would show two black pros who were denied the chance to compete in the 1948 Richmond Open because of the color of their skin.

And as a result, it was there where one of those two men, Bill Spiller, opened the struggle to change that order of things.[1]

— Al Barkow, originally
printed in Golf World

Sports writers are storytellers. They tell action stories and human interest stories about real people. They share information in the form of facts, quotations and numbers, but their ultimate goal is to create detailed pictures of athletes as human beings with whom readers and viewers can identify. As in the above feature story lead, they explain events and explore issues.

To a true sports storyteller, it's not enough to say who won, who lost and what the score was. The storyteller focuses on how people interacted to reach that end and uses descriptive details to bring the event to life. To decide what makes the event worth a story, the sports writer considers its news value to the audience. On the 60th anniversary of Bill Spiller's "struggle to change that order of things," Al Barkow decided it was time to tell his story.

What makes Spiller's story news now? It has conflict, a timely anniversary, prominence, consequence and human interest. And for golfers and minorities everywhere, it has emotional proximity. All the values that make a sports story newsworthy are wrapped up in the story of a black man who sued the PGA of America (not today's PGA Tour, which did not exist at that time) for $315,000 because its constitution allowed membership only to Caucasians.

SPORTS NEWS VALUES

- Conflict.
- Timeliness.
- Prominence.
- Proximity.
- Consequence or impact.
- Human interest.
- Unusualness.

Sports and news share a common set of values that turn stories into news to a specific, identifiable audience. The values are the same in print, on air and online. Sports fans want to read and hear about their favorite teams. They're interested in stories about games they've seen to compare their ideas of what happened during play and what it means to the team through the eyes of the players and coaches. Fans also want to know about the games they've missed and how those performances will affect their seasons. They want to know more about their favorite athlete's life away from sports. Sometimes they just want to see or hear their child's name in the news.

Conflict

- Who played?
- Who won?

PHOTO 5.1
Football is a classic example of the "conflict" news value with two sides squaring off to see who will be the winner.
iStock Essentials/ActionPics

- Was someone injured?
- Was personal conflict involved?
- Was a rule or law broken?

Sports competitions are based on conflict: two or more competitors, one winner. A record holder is out to beat his or her personal best. A competitor develops a health problem. Every sport from curling to beach volleyball has its version of the Masters Golf Tournament, Wimbledon, the Final Four or the World Series.

Competitive eating champion Takeru Kobayashi won the Cadillac of competitive eating matches, Nathan's Famous Hot Dog Eating Contest, six years in a row. The seventh year, Kobayashi swallowed 63 hot dogs and buns in the allotted 12 minutes, beating his own record of 56 the year before, but it wasn't good enough. He lost the title to Joey Chestnut, who downed 66 dogs in the same time to win the contest.

Game coverage describes the conflict and breaks it down into individual plays, moments of heartbreaking defeat, and dramatic, adrenalin-pumping victory. Preseason and pregame stories anticipate the conflict, analyze the players and predict the outcome based on previous contests and stats. Postseason and postgame stories analyze the conflict, rehash the coaching calls and possibly tease the fans with predictions about what the future holds for key players or opponents.

Conflict also makes news off the field or court. A player is charged with a crime. An unpopular coaching change is made. An athlete is involved in an accident. Basketball star Kobe Bryant faced rape charges, and the story made headlines for months before the case was dismissed. When Tour de France winner Floyd Landis was determined to have used performance-enhancing drugs during the race, both the Tour's and Landis' reputations suffered.

Timeliness
- When did or will the event happen?
- When will the audience know about the story?
- What is the deadline?
- What does the audience know about the subject before seeing this story?
- Is this new information or an update to an existing story?

As a news value, timeliness is the first time a story is published or broadcast. The same story is not timely again unless new information is added. The continuous deadlines of online media and live coverage have boosted timeliness from anything that's happened since the last edition or newscast to what's happening in real 24/7 time.

Timeliness may also be seasonal. A preseason story is timely shortly before play for that sport's season begins. Signings, training camps, playoffs and the Super Bowl are subjects for seasonally timely stories.

Timeliness is relevant to the medium and influences the perspective from which the story is presented. Timeliness for newspapers can be as little as an hour or as long as a week for the next edition. Timeliness for broadcast is live coverage, the next regularly scheduled newscast, or, if the news is important enough, "We interrupt this broadcast for . . . ."

Timeliness for online stories is immediate, with updates as often as new information becomes available. Reporters and bloggers upload game commentary in the online equivalent of play-by-play. Each story and update is marked with the exact time it was posted.

Deadline differences dictate content differences. A game played tonight will be a game story on tonight's sportscast. The same game online has been updated several times during the game with a complete story as soon as it's over and another update after interviews with the coaches and players. Tomorrow's newspaper will carry a detailed game story with quotes from the coaches, statistics and an analysis of how this game changes the season for the team or the rankings for the tournament.

Consider these leads for the same story collected from print, broadcast and online. The indication of when the event happened and the content varies with each medium's deadline. The time of the announcement and the names of the candidates for an individual award were released in advance so reporters had time to gather background for the story before the moment the winner was announced.

For example, following the 6 p.m. ceremony in New York where the winner of the highest honor awarded to a college-level female athlete, the Honda-Broderick Cup, was announced, usatoday.com posted this lead at 6:36 p.m. (ET) Monday:

> Nebraska volleyball star Sarah Pavan maintained a 4.0 grade-point average in biochemistry while leading the Cornhuskers to a 33-1 season and the NCAA title. Those achievements earned the junior from Kitchener, Ontario, the 31st annual Honda-Broderick Cup as the nation's female college athlete of the year Monday.[2]

At 7:18 p.m. (ET) Monday, after the post-announcement interview or news conference, usatoday.com updated the lead to reflect Pavan's response:

> Nebraska volleyball player Sarah Pavan was shocked to win the Honda-Broderick Cup, which was announced Monday in New York.[3]

Viewers of the 10 p.m. (CT) local sports report in Nebraska Monday heard this lead:

> Even before she was named Collegiate Woman Athlete of the Year, University of Nebraska volleyball player Sarah Pavan had already won some great honors. Pavan helped lead the Huskers to the National Championship and was selected NCAA Volleyball Player of the Year and the Academic All-American Player of the Year.
>
> Today Pavan won the Honda-Broderick Cup Award. . . .[4]

A central Nebraska daily newspaper ran this lead Tuesday afternoon:

> She has achieved "celebrity status" in Nebraska, UNL volleyball coach John Cook said.

"When she shows up to speak to grade school kids in her [Nebraska] sweats, the kids shut up and listen."

Nebraska's Sarah Pavan on Monday won the Honda-Broderick Cup becoming the nation's female athlete of the year and the first Nebraska athlete to be named in the 31-year history of the award.

Since coming to UNL from Kitchener, Ontario, the 6-5 junior has led the team to three national titles. . . .[5]

Prominence

- Will people recognize the name of the person or team?
- Is the person or event locally, nationally or internationally known?
- Is the championship or award commonly recognized and respected?

Prominence is having name recognition among the audience. Local athletes have prominence in their communities' media, professional teams and athletes have national prominence, Tiger Woods and LeBron James have international prominence and make news both on the course or court and off, just because people — those who follow sports and those who do not — know their names.

A story about tennis phenom Serena Williams giving birth to a daughter is news because it's happening to a well-known sports figure, not because it is about sports or because no one has ever done it before.

Michael Phelps was just another promising swimmer before he gained prominence as an Olympic superstar. Now the most successful and most decorated Olympian ever, he boasts a collection of 28 gold medals.

Few recognized the name Lance Armstrong before he won the Tour de France in 1999, but by the time he won his seventh consecutive Tour, Armstrong had become an internationally prominent athlete. When he was later proven to have used performance-enhancing drugs and was stripped of all his titles, his name became news again.

At age 17, Hawaiian golfer Michelle Wie was the first woman named to Sports Illustrated's annual list of the 50 top-earning American athletes. Wie was No. 22.

Proximity

- Did the event take place close to home?
- Were people the audience knows involved?
- Does the local audience have an emotional connection to a story happening elsewhere?

Proximity is nearness in place, time or allegiance, and it may be geographical or emotional. Sporting events that happen in your community and involve people your audience knows are news in your community's media. College teams have proximity in the state or region. Professional teams have local proximity in their hometowns and national proximity because their loyal fans are dispersed throughout the country and their games are broadcast regularly.

For years, the Boise State Broncos won a few and lost a few on the famous blue artificial playing surface in Bronco Stadium in front of loyal hometown fans. The Idaho Statesman covered Bronco games and charted their rise to win the Western Athletic Conference championship five times. Then came the season when, with a first-year head coach and a perfect record, they earned a trip to the Fiesta Bowl. More than 20,000 fans followed the Broncos to Arizona, but, for the fans at home watching their Broncos face-off against the Oklahoma Sooners on television or online, the game had emotional proximity. Even though the game was a thousand miles away, they were there in spirit to see their team become the Fiesta Bowl champion in a 43-42 upset in overtime.

Consequence or Impact

- What will change as a result of this?
- How many people will be affected?
- Will this action result in legal, financial, emotional or ethical change for players, teams or fans?

Consequence is gauged by the impact an action or change will have on a number of people, and consequence stories explain the impact so people will understand what it means to them. Talk shows and blogs often focus discussion on the possible impact of an action by an individual or a governing organization.

A rules change, a policy shift, a salary negotiation or a change in ticket prices has the potential to change behavior or circumstance far beyond the initial act. If ticket prices go up, some fans may attend fewer games or not purchase the season tickets they have always had. The program loses income, the concessionaires sell fewer hot dogs, the printer prints fewer tickets and employees collect less trash in less time. Eventually people lose jobs, and the program has to make cuts because the dollars aren't coming in to cover expenses.

On the other hand, the university decides to expand the stadium by adding 20,000 seats by next season. That certainly means more tickets sold, probably at a higher price, more pizza and popcorn consumed, more trash generated and maybe even more games added to the schedule. More people are hired to provide security and clean up after the game.

That's an extreme example, but reactions and repercussions invariably follow any change, and it's the reporter's job to keep the public informed of the impact beyond the official action.

Human Interest
- Does this story tug at the heartstrings?
- Is this story about personal emotional trauma or triumph?
- What has the athlete overcome or the family sacrificed?
- How does an athlete or coach spend time away from work or sports?

The human interest value fills people's natural curiosity about other people. From pictures on cave walls to text messaging and Instagrams, human beings have communicated to learn how others think, feel, overcome obstacles and succeed. Human interest stories stir emotions and make people feel the urge to take action, if only by blogging their opinions and support.

For instance, bloggers sided with Oscar Pistorius, a double amputee with a big goal, after he appeared on ABC's morning news show. Pistorius, a sprinter dubbed "the blade runner" because of the shape of his prosthetic legs, wanted to run in the Olympics in 2008.

He had already earned gold medals and set records in the 100-meter, 200-meter and 400-meter races at Paralympics competitions. But when the South African athlete announced that he intended to try out for the Olympics, the International Association of Athletics Federations said Pistorius' prosthetic limbs might give him an advantage over runners with legs and proposed a rule that would prohibit him from participating in Olympic competition.

Approximately 85 percent of readers who wrote comments about the abcnews.com story in the two weeks after it was posted sided with Pistorius, commending his accomplishments and defending his right to compete against "able-bodied" athletes in the summer Olympics.

In player profiles, sidebars and sports features, readers and viewers expect to hear the human interest side of the story: whose side of the field the grandmother sits on when she has a grandchild on each team, what kind of therapy it took to rehab a player's injury, how it feels to play the last game of a collegiate career, what a player's hobbies and favorite charities are, how a man with prosthetic legs reacts when he's told he's not allowed to compete in the Olympics.

The IAAF ruled Pistorius ineligible to compete in the Olympics because "his carbon fiber blades give him a mechanical advantage. The IAAF based its decision on studies by German professor Gert-Peter Brueggemann, who said the J-shaped 'cheetah' blades were energy efficient."[6]

"I was pretty surprised by the outcome . . . and I was pretty disappointed," Pistorius said.

This time, those who posted comments on abcnews.com were divided almost evenly between Pistorius' supporters and those who sided with the committee or commented on related issues. In the end, the Court of Arbitration for Sport overturned the IAAF ruling and said Pistorius could compete in the Olympic games if he qualified for the team. Pistorius failed to qualify. He went on to triple-gold-medal in the 100-meter dash, 200-meter dash and 400-meter dash in the Beijing Paralympic Games and to qualify for the Olympic team in 2012.

Unusualness

- Is this story out of the ordinary on sports pages?
- Has this rarely or never happened before?
- Is it so unusual that people will be amused or entertained by it?

Most of the starters in a car race eventually cross the finish line with four tires on the track. That's why when NASCAR driver Clint Bowyer's No. 7 Chevrolet slid across the finish line upside down and on fire at the Daytona 500, it was unusual. Even though Bowyer placed 18th, his finish was the most visual image to emerge from the race and stole the headlines from winner and teammate Kevin Harvick.

French tennis player Tatiana Golovin's choice to wear red shorts during play at Wimbledon was unusual enough to attract attention from the audience, the referee and the media. The referee consulted the rulebook before declaring the red shorts underwear — not a visible part of Golovin's white tennis dress — and therefore acceptable attire for Wimbledon's all-white dress code.

A neighbor called the Laramie police at 7 a.m. to complain that the music the University of Wyoming football players were playing through the new jumbotron in the stadium during their early morning practice was too loud. Campus police were able to get the music turned down. A player tweeted, "Who calls the police on their football team?"

PHOTO 5.2
This player's tennis dress meets Wimbledon's strict all-white dress code.
iStock Essentials/jacoblund

FEATURE STORIES

Features are timeless human-interest stories that tell about people doing something special or out of the ordinary, stories that entertain as they inform. The best feature stories tug at the heartstrings. They are most often based on human interest or unusual news values.

ADVANCE STORIES

Advance, or pregame, stories prepare readers for what they may see during a sporting event.

Advance stories

- Are timely.
- Appear a day or two before the event.

Lead

- Direct.
- 5 Ws and an H.

Structure

- Inverted pyramid or Model T.

Content*

- Name of event (U.S. Tennis Open, Rose Bowl, Final Four).
- Place and time of event.
- Names of opponents, conference, division.
- Names, accomplishments of key players.
- Comments from the coaches, players.
- Strategies or plays to expect.
- Strengths, weaknesses of opponents.
- History of rivalry.
- Results of previous competitions.
- Season records, past and present.

*Order of content will vary with story

LEADS

The lead is the beginning of a media story. It sets the scene and tells readers and viewers what happened. On a sports news story, the lead introduces the teams, players, competition and score, and at least hints at how play led to the outcome. On a sports feature, the lead focuses on the person or topic, drawing the audience in with examples, anecdotes, word pictures or an unusual circumstance.

A well-written lead on a well-organized story assures readers that no matter where they exit the story, even after the first paragraph or two, they will have enough information to know what happened.

News values help sports writers determine the lead and structure for their stories. If a fight breaks out on the court, the conflict will almost certainly be the lead. If a record is broken, the consequence or impact is likely to be the lead. If it's a game story, timeliness (when) will be a value, but more important, the result of the conflict — the score — will be in the lead. So will prominence (who), and maybe the human interest. If a well-known player is involved, whether it's a game story or a news story, the name (prominence) will be in the lead, usually connected to another news value such as conflict or consequence.

Think of the lead as a basketball at the moment it reaches the high point of the official's toss. At that moment, all eyes are on the ball. Fans hold their breath for a millisecond. Arms stretch, fingertips poised to direct the ball as it descends. Eyes, then bodies, turn and follow the ball into play. At that moment no one knows who will win, what the score will be or who will be injured or foul out. What they do know is that an unpredictable sequence of plays will become a game and their team has a chance to win.

The tipoff is when the real story begins. Some of the fans will watch every play intently. Some will watch for a quarter, then go out for popcorn, come back, go out to get a drink, come back. Some will check their cellphones to see what the bloggers are saying. Some will watch the cheerleaders, the people in the next row, the instant replays or the scoreboard more than the game. Some will leave and never return.

Readers and viewers focus on the lead of a game story with just as much interest and intensity as they did the basketball as it went into the air to start the game. The lead should give them enough information so they know what game they're reading about, and it should create enough intrigue that they want to read or hear more. But readers and viewers are like fans at a game. Some will read or listen to every word. Some will pay attention for a few paragraphs or comments before they go out for popcorn. Some will leave and never return.

The major difference between a toss and a lead is that the toss is only the beginning of something. The lead also reveals the outcome. Game story leads tell the end first, but the best ones tell it in such a way that even someone who saw or listened to the game will be curious enough to pay attention.

Here's how Shirley Povich of the Washington Post & Times Herald captured readers' attention for a story about a 1956 World Series game:

> The million-to-one shot came in. Hell froze over. A month of Sundays hit the calendar. Don Larsen today pitched a no-hit, no-run, no-man-reach-first game in a World Series.[7]

Writing the Lead

Readers will decide in seven to 14 words whether to read on or move on. That makes writing the lead one of the biggest challenges a sports writer faces.

The lead sets the tone for the story. It must convey enough information to tease readers and viewers into the story while not giving away so much that they are content to know who played, who won and what the score was.

The writer's goal is to craft a lead that exudes the importance and energy of the event. An allusion lead written in 1924 by New York Herald Tribune sports writer Grantland Rice to describe the Notre Dame-Army football game is considered by many to be the most famous lead in sports-writing history.

Rice captures the tension and energy of not-just-another-football-game by casting it in deep historic shadows where ominous mounted personas with cyclonic power ride onto the battlefield to challenge a fighting army.

> Outlined against a blue-gray October sky, the Four Horsemen rode again. In dramatic lore they are known as Famine, Pestilence, Destruction and Death. These are only aliases. Their real names are Stuhldreher, Miller, Crowley and Layden. They formed the crest of the South Bend cyclone before which another fighting Army football team was swept over the precipice at the Polo Grounds yesterday afternoon as 55,000 spectators peered down on the bewildering panorama spread on the green plain below.[8]

Notre Dame defeated Army 13-7 that day. Coached by Knute Rockne and led by the four backs who played from 1922 to 1924, Notre Dame went on to a 10-0 season. Rockne's student publicity aide arranged a photo of the four uniformed players mounted on horses. The photo was picked up by the wire services, cementing Rice's lead and the Four Horsemen in the annals of sports-writing history.

PHOTO 5.3
A Notre Dame student publicity aide staged a photo of the four players who came to be known as the "Four Horsemen of Notre Dame." L-R: Don Miller, Elmer Layden, Jim Crowley and Harry Stuhldreher. The photo became the prototype for this statute.
Associated Press.

Sometimes the lead is written first. Sometimes it is written last.

When sports reporters are covering a game or a news conference and have short deadlines following the event to file the story, they often write the body of the story (B copy) as the game unfolds and add the lead at the conclusion of the action.

When writer's block strikes, as it does for every writer at some time, the cure may be to write the rest of the story. The lead usually reveals itself as the story develops. A forced or contrived lead always sounds like what it is: the writer attempting to make the story fit the lead instead of the lead setting up the story.

The job of the lead is to:

- Capture the attention of the audience and make them want to know more.
- Establish the theme or essence of the story.
- Reflect the tension and energy of the event.
- Summarize key information.

Summarizing the key information is easy once the reporter identifies the 5 Ws and an H:

Who   =   the UC Irvine Anteaters
What   =   defeated Arizona State 8-7
Where   =   College World Series
When   =   Tuesday
Why   =   the Anteaters are serious about winning a national championship
How   =   in their final at-bat in the tenth inning

Some of this information is known before the game begins, but some isn't known until it ends. Once the facts are identified, compare them to the news values. Which component has the highest news value to the audience? Is a prominent person or team playing? Was it the tournament championship game? Was there a key play that clinched the game?

From this the reporter should be able to summarize the story in a sentence or two, beginning with the word or words with the most audience appeal.

> The UC Irvine Anteaters won in their fi-
> nal at-bat for the third time in four games
> on Tuesday night, knocking off Arizona
> State 8-7 in 10 innings in an elimination
> game at the College World Series.[9]

The why and the how are included in this lead, but often they are found in the next paragraph or two. Seldom is the day of the event the factor with the most audience appeal, but it should be in the lead, as it is in AP writer Eric Olson's story. Olson could have written:

> Tuesday night the UC Irvine Anteaters
> defeated Arizona State 8-7 in 10 innings
> in a College World Series elimination
> game.

Or he could have written:

> Tuesday's College World Series elimi-
> nation game went 10 innings before the
> UC Irvine Anteaters sent Arizona State
> home with a loss.

In the first example, Tuesday night is an accurate descriptor. In the second example, it is not correct if more than one game was played on Tuesday.

Both are acceptable leads, but in neither case is Tuesday the most important or engaging word. If the reader's eye skips to Anteaters or College World Series, there's a chance that reader will stay with the story at least long enough to read the lead.

Two Types of Leads

Leads fit into two general categories: direct and delayed. The lead can be as short as the first sentence of a story, or it can be as long as several paragraphs. Advances, gamers and briefs usually have short, direct leads while features, profiles and in-depth stories are more likely to have longer, delayed leads. But they're not mutually exclusive: Gamers may have delayed leads and in-depth stories may have direct leads.

Direct Leads

Direct leads, also called summary leads, are timely and present information quickly. If readers stopped at the end of a direct lead, they would know who played, who won, what the score was and where and when the event happened.

Game story reporters on deadline use direct leads because they're quick and easy to compose. Readers and listeners like direct leads because all the key information is readily available to help them decide whether to continue with the story or move on to the next. Editors like direct leads because they know if there's not enough room for the whole story, it can be shortened from the bottom without losing important facts or a conclusion necessary to the understanding of the story.

Direct leads are appropriate for most sports stories. They are also used in news stories about trends in sports, advances in sports medicine, sports and politics or government, or sports and the courts. These stories are more likely to appear on news pages, where direct leads dominate, than among the gamers, sidebars and box scores on the sports pages. Direct leads are also standard for the first story posted online as a game ends and newspaper stories written on tight deadlines.

A complaint about direct leads is that they all begin to sound like fill-in-the-blank boilerplate. The last thing readers want in a sports story is copy that's dull and boring. If it's an important game, the first thing they want to know is who won. One way to pique curiosity is to add a short teaser sentence that entices viewers or readers to stick with it to find out what the reporter knows that they don't.

The College World Series story about the Anteaters' win ran on the AP wire with this lead:

> That team with the funny nickname is serious about winning a national championship.
>
> The UC Irvine Anteaters won in their final at-bat for the third time in four games on Tuesday night, knock-

ing off Arizona State 8-7 in 10 innings
in an elimination game at the College
World Series.

Now it is clear why winning the game was so critical and how hard the Anteaters
had played to reach this point.

Delayed Leads

Leads that do not summarize the event immediately are called delayed leads. Delayed leads are good for stories that could run any time. They use visual descriptions and emotional appeals to show the subject of a profile doing something unrelated to sports or to introduce the subject of a sports feature. In a delayed lead, the 5 Ws and an H are not all clear until several sentences, even paragraphs, into the story.

A delayed lead may take the form of an anecdote, a short, presumably true story with a point to make about the subject. The lead might set up a scene that invites readers or viewers to imagine themselves becoming part of it, or it might create a portrait of the subject engaged in some activity. The point of the anecdote may be completed in the lead or not revealed until the end of the story, but the lead should transition into the body of the story by telling the reader what focus the story is going to take.

PHOTO 5.4
Baseball teams of all ages make news playing the great American sport.
iStock Essentials/1PGGutenbergUKLtd

FEATURE STORIES

Features are timeless human-interest stories that tell about people doing something special, or out-or-the-ordinary stories that entertain as they inform. The best feature stories tug at the heartstrings.

Features may

- Stand alone or run as a sidebar to a news story.
- Run any time.
- Be hooked to news, season or proximity.
- Inform, educate or entertain.
- Profile a person.
- Explore innovations, trends or issues.

Lead

- Most often delayed.
- Anecdote, picture that sets up the story.
- 5 Ws and an H.

Structure

- Circular, tells a story.
- Longer; space planned ahead of time.
- Quotations: subject, sources tell story.
- Conclusion usually ties back to lead.

Language

- Picture words show subject, setting.
- News story: fact and observation, not opinion or analysis.

Al Barkow's lead on "One Man's Mission" at the beginning of this chapter is an anecdote that transports the reader into the men's locker room at the Richmond Country Club. Hanging on the wall are photographs of golf greats Sam Snead, Toney Penna, George Schoux and E.J. "Dutch" Harrison when they won the Richmond Open more than 60 years ago.

Then Barkow introduces the intrigue: the photo that was never taken of two black men denied the chance to compete in the Richmond Open because of a membership rule allowing only Caucasians to play in PGA of America-sponsored events. Suddenly the story isn't about a picturesque golf course across the bay from San Francisco; it's about Bill Spiller and his crusade to get the rules changed.

An anecdote sets up the following story about one of the nation's best 70-and-over slow-pitch softball teams. It transports readers to the field where they feel the summer heat, meet the players and ultimately want to stay to watch the game.

> LIBERTY, Mo. — Think heat, motion-stifling, odor-producing, nap-inspiring heat. Think of sitting in an attic in the Sahara with a space heater under your rump. Think of eating Grandma's chili with her wool quilt over your head.
>
> Records will show the temperature on July 6 in this Kansas City suburb topped out at 93, but if you think it was a day to swing a bat instead of playing pinochle down at the coffee shop, somebody poured a few shots of something in your chili.
>
> Think heat, Great Depression-era heat. You can ask the guys on the diamond about that kind of heat. They're primary sources. They started playing ball in that heat in the 1930s and '40s when baseball was the thing.
>
> Most never really stopped.
>
> "You know every spring the robins come hopping along," said 71-year-old Lee Leriger of Norfolk. "Well, it's the same thing with us. We'll play 'til we can't."
>
> They call themselves the Omaha Spirit and they don't just play, they win enough to earn distinction as one of the nation's best 70-and-over slow-pitch softball teams.[10]
>
> — Dirk Chatelain, Omaha World-Herald. Copyright 2008. All rights reserved.

NUT GRAF

The nut graf is the sentence or paragraph that tells the reader what the story is about and what slant the writer will take. In the slow-pitch softball lead, it is the last paragraph. Readers now know the story will be about a team of men age 70 and older preparing to compete in a national tournament, and it will have a lighthearted tone.

The nut graf may be the first sentence in a story with a direct lead, or, as in the Bill Spiller and slow-pitch softball stories, it may be the sixth or seventh paragraph in a feature story with a delayed lead. If a story does not have a clear nut graf, the reader will become confused by the story or lose interest after a few paragraphs.

FINDING THE NUT GRAF

Delayed

If you listened closely to the women's basketball games this week, some say, you could actually hear the records breaking.

En route to a 20-3 season, the Blue Jays were led by senior co-captain Tamara Bunner who broke the school's 26-year-old career scoring record with 1,967.

Senior Jeanne Egan smashed the record for rebounds in a season with 311 for an average of 11.6 per game.

Along the way, the team played some heart-stopping games including Friday's conference tournament championship match that ended the Tigers' season.

With the score tied and 1.7 seconds remaining, a three-pointer by Bunner put the Blue Jays up 59-56 for the championship.

Direct

The Wildcat freshmen came up with a clutch performance for the women's basketball team during Wednesday's 69-64 win over conference rival Sundown State.

The win keeps the No. 8 Wildcats in a tie atop the conference standings, while No. 11 Sundown drops two games back.

"They kept their heads about them," coach Abby Wood said of the freshmen.

"They hit some free throws and took care of business. Next time we're in that situation, they should be less nervous."

Try the "cut" test on these stories to find the nut graf. Starting at the bottom, cut one paragraph at a time until no more can be cut without losing information necessary to understanding the stories.

Leads to Avoid

Asking a question would seem an easy way to pull readers into a story. Reporters formulate questions to ask before interviewing sources or to answer before beginning to write a story. Readers have the same questions, but they expect answers from the reporter, not more questions. It's too easy for a reader to answer a question with "yes," "no" or "I don't care," and move on without reading the answer the reporter worked so hard to find.

Readers like to know what people said, and that makes quotations tempting to use as leads. Sometimes a source puts the whole story, the intrigue, in one colorful, concise sentence, and it is worth risking a quotation to introduce a delayed lead. Finding a quote that captures the essence of the story without an introduction is rare. It's better to use the quotations to embellish the lead.

If the lead is a quotation, use the next sentence to explain the situation and add enough facts so the reader knows why the quotation is significant. In this example, the writer used the quotation first to capture some of the anguish and disappointment team members might be feeling, but it would also have explained the lead if it had followed the first sentence.

> "It's frustrating. But it is what it is. That's what I told them. . . . It's gonna hurt," Jaguars coach Nathelle Skiles said.
> The Cardinals flew into the Sports Center on Saturday and squeaked out a 72-70 victory over a Jaguar team desperate for a conference win.

STORY STRUCTURE

Sports writers use the same structure patterns as news writers to organize stories. Once the facts have been identified, the background research done and the sources interviewed, the writer plans how to tell the story.

Inverted Pyramid

The most used organization pattern for media stories is the inverted pyramid. An unwieldy, top-heavy triangle looking more like a diamond solitaire than a pyramid, the image is an appropriate way to show the most-important-to-least-important arrangement of information in a news story. Sports news stories, game stories and some features and sidebars use the inverted pyramid (figure 5.1) because of its reader-friendly organization that allows the reader to stop at any point after the lead while still knowing what the story is about.

GAME STORIES

Game stories tell readers what the reporter saw and what the numbers show happened at the game.

Game stories
- Are timely.
- Appear soon after the event.

Lead
- Direct.
- 5 Ws and an H.

Structure
- Inverted pyramid or Model T.

Content*
- Score.
- Name of event, e.g., U.S. Tennis Open.
- Names of opponents, conference, division.
- Specific location of event.
- Key plays, key players' impact.
- Unexpected factors affecting outcome: injuries, penalties, weather.
- Comments from coaches, players.
- Impact of strategies or plays executed.
- Strengths, weaknesses of opponents.
- Results of previous competition.
- Season records, past and present.
- Next contest if significant, e.g., tournament.

*Order of content will vary with story.

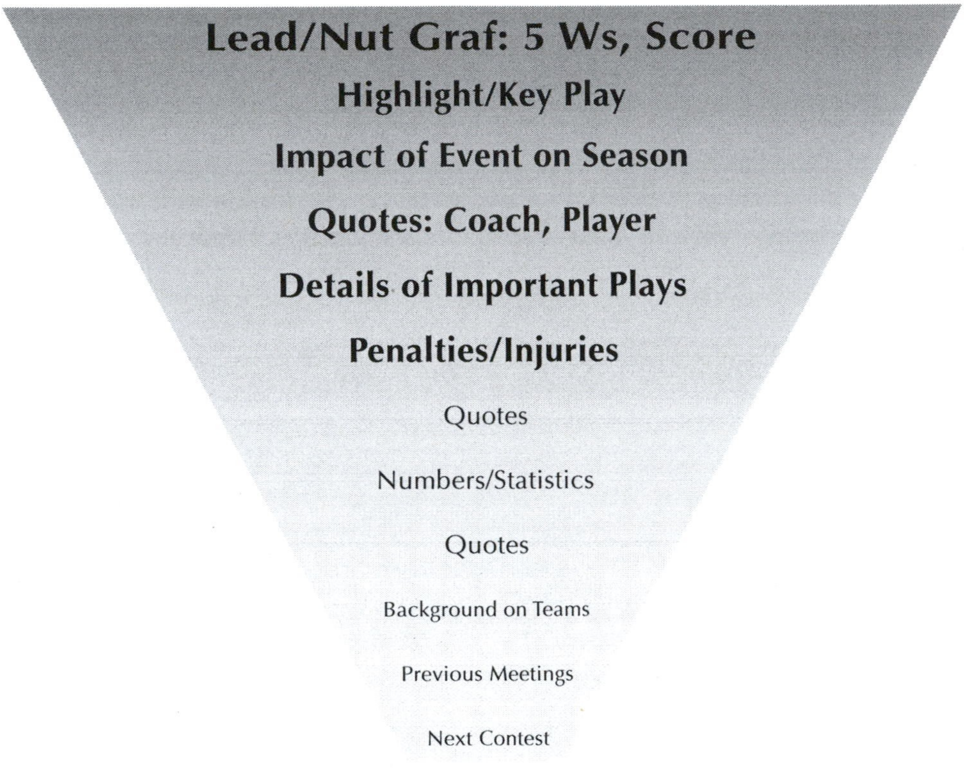

Lead/Nut Graf: 5 Ws, Score

Highlight/Key Play

Impact of Event on Season

Quotes: Coach, Player

Details of Important Plays

Penalties/Injuries

Quotes

Numbers/Statistics

Quotes

Background on Teams

Previous Meetings

Next Contest

*Order of information will vary with story

FIGURE 5.1
Inverted Pyramid
Graphic by Isaiah May

"Who won?" and "What was the score?" are the first questions asked by someone who hasn't yet heard about the game. After they know the end of the story — the score — they may ask, "What happened?" Most people would tell the story beginning from the end and moving through the game from highlight to highlight in a descending order of importance as they remember it. You might tell the story this way:

Did you see that game? Wow! Tied with 2 seconds on the clock!

The Dogs were down 13-7 with 1:02 to go, and then they pulled a fancy zig-zag play nobody's seen before — Brooks passed to Pratt, and he actually caught it on the 30. He tossed it off to Wood — he hasn't caught anything all season, but he was awesome — just grabbed it out of the air like it was nothing! Then he has to get rid of it before they take him out.

So he aims in the direction of the end zone and lets it fly. You shoulda' seen it! Doerr was standing there with his hands up and this smirk on his face just like he was waiting for it all the time.

No pressure on Kramer! He laid one on that pigskin, dead center on the posts, his best kick all season, puts us up 14-13. Man, our Dogs barked all the way home!

If you were writing the story, your lead might be something like this:

> Jack Kramer's extra-point kick was good. Some might even say perfect.
>
> With two seconds left on the Memorial Stadium clock, Kramer slipped in the final point, giving the University Dogs a 14-13 win over the College Wildcats on Saturday.

Subsequent paragraphs, in the appropriate order of importance to the audience, would

- Explain the new play.
- Quote the coach on the play and on the performance of key players.
- Quote players who participated in the touchdown and extra point plays.
- Review earlier scoring.
- Show how this game affects both teams on the season.
- Wrap with a look back at Kramer's extra-point kick or ahead to next week.

Most readers already know who won and may even have seen the game or television footage of the last play before they read the story. But sports fans are insatiable, especially if their team is winning. It doesn't matter how many times they've seen it or read it, they'll do it again, sometimes for years. They're ravenous media consumers where their favorite teams are concerned. They want to relive the high points of each game again and again and to know what the coach said, how Kramer felt as his toe connected with the ball and what fans thought about the last-minute turnaround their team finessed.

That's the concept illustrated by the inverted pyramid organization pattern. The first questions fans would ask are the most important to them and should form the base upon which the rest of the story is built. Without a solid base, a pyramid would not stand. Without a solid lead, the story will not make sense. The base of the story is at the top with the supporting information flowing from a most-interesting-to-the-largest-number-of-people lead to the least-interesting-to-the-largest-number-of-people at the end.

Readers, reporters and editors like inverted pyramid stories because they are quick and efficient to read, to write and to place on the page. The information of most inter-

est to the most people is in the first paragraphs or on the first screen. The least necessary information is at the end so the reader who doesn't scroll to the second screen
won't miss a key point. A print or online inverted pyramid story can be cut from the
bottom if space is limited without losing vital information.

Sports reporters like the inverted pyramid for the same reasons and more. It works
for game stories and news briefs. Sports reporters working on short deadlines or with
continuous online updates find the pattern especially helpful because they can start the
story during the event and insert information anywhere in the story as it becomes available. The lead changes as the story develops, but it isn't complete until the clock runs out.

Inverted Pyramid Online: Model T Organization

Online readers scan for chunks of information, according to converged media writing expert Janet Kolodzy.[11] The pyramid becomes a stack of blocks separated by white
space descending from a larger square or rectangle representing the lead. Each chunk
may stand alone, presenting a small part of the story but being a complete thought in
itself for readers who just want to scan the page for interesting tidbits.

A stripped-down version of the inverted pyramid, the Model T organization pattern introduced by MSNBC.com (figure 5.2), is popular with online news writers.

Direct Lead/Nut Graf: 5 Ws and an H, Score

Highlight or
Key Play

Quotes from
Coach, Player

Details/Facts

Quote

Statistics/Numbers

Background

Next Meeting

*Order of information will vary with story

FIGURE 5.2
Model T
Graphic by Isaiah May

Online readers move quickly from story to story, spending only seconds deciding whether to read anything more than the lead. A direct lead forms the horizontal top of the T. It gives the reader a quick overview of the story and a reason to keep reading. The vertical line represents the rest of the story told in whatever order best supports the lead.

FOLLOW-UP STORIES

Follow-up stories reflect upon the game and analyze the results. They focus on players, strategy and the long-term impact of the event.

Follow-Up Stories
- Are timely.
- Appear a day or two after the event.

Lead
- Direct or delayed.
- May be reflective or anecdotal.
- 5 Ws and an H.

Structure
- Inverted pyramid or Model T.
- Circular.

Content/Analysis*
- Recap of score, occasion, location.
- Name of event, e.g., U.S. Tennis Open.
- Names of opponents, conference, division.
- Reflective response by coaches, players.
- Key plays, key players' impact.
- Unexpected factors affecting outcome: injuries, penalties, weather.
- Impact of strategies or plays executed.
- Strengths, weaknesses of opponents.
- Effect on teams' seasons.
- Next contest if significant, e.g., tournament.

*Order of content will vary with story

Circular Story Structure

Broadcast media predominantly use a circular organization pattern (figure 5.3) for their stories. Each story has a beginning, a middle and an end, and it must tell the whole story in a strictly controlled time. Game stories, for instance, begin with a direct lead, add details or video and sound bites in the middle, and end with a wrap that ties content back to the lead to complete the story line. The wrap might anticipate the next step, such as when the teams will meet again, or it might restate the outcome of the event or finish a theme begun in the lead. If circular stories need to be shortened, they must be carefully edited in the middle so the tie-back is not lost.

The circular pattern is also good for features and profiles in all media. Because features and profiles are planned ahead and can run most any day, they can be longer and still run without editing for length. Features and profiles look and sound like short stories because of their delayed leads and circular structure, so readers anticipate an ending. They are disappointed if the story ends abruptly without some conclusion. The ending does not have to wrap up the plot line; it can just refer back to something

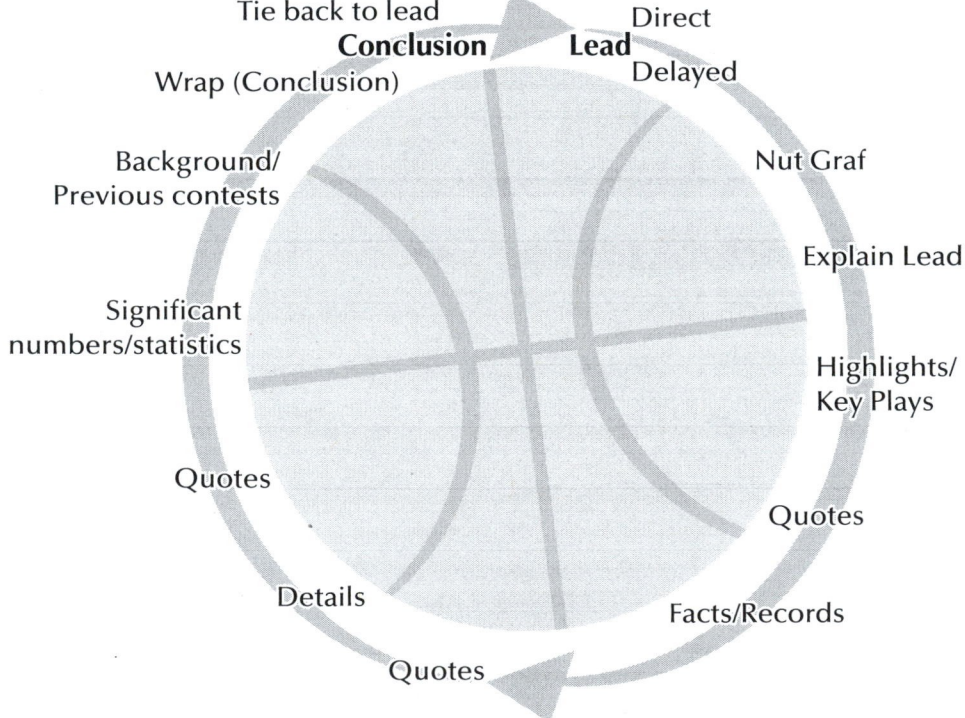

Order of information will vary with story

FIGURE 5.3
Circular Story Structure
Graphic by Isaiah May

in the lead. The lead should not give away the ending if the writer chooses an organization pattern that leads to a conclusion.

One college reporter circled the track post-season story this way:

P. I. T.

Passion. Intensity. Team.

P.I.T. became the mantra for the indoor and outdoor track teams this season. Few on the team actually thought this acronym, designed to inspire individuals and create team unity, would really produce results.

However, as the season progressed, it seemed this new mentality helped propel the athletes to record-breaking heights.

Together, nine members of the track teams broke 14 school records, two members were named conference athletes of the week, and 13 earned All-American status. [Body of story removed.]

Sounds like the P.I.T. crew doesn't need much fine-tuning.[12]

COLUMNS

Columns and editorials provide the personality and passion that news reporting doesn't show, according to Tim Harrower in "Inside Reporting."[13]

It's OK to take a position if you're a columnist. It's acceptable to analyze and criticize. It's the one place you can use your imagination, paint pictures, create a persona, say what you think — based on the facts — and still be respected as a sports journalist. Becoming the staff columnist is the pinnacle of sports writing, and the title has to be earned.

Columns are the most read part of the sports page. Readers and viewers find sports columns appealing because they add color, interest and perspective to the sports section. Fans like to know what those on the inside, the columnists, think. They're also attracted to columns with a voice, a style, a personality that comes through consistently in a columnist's writing. Readers or viewers who identify with a columnist become regular followers and begin to think of the columnist as a friend, someone who shares similar ideas or makes them chuckle. Mike Babcock, freelance sports writer and columnist, said,

When you're a reporter, your words have an impact on your audience. Columnists especially. People listen to you. I would never call for the firing of a coach, because it's not my place. Readers believe what they read. It's not my job to tell them what to do.[14]

Sports writers who know their beats and their communities well have long-term familiarity with their audience and with their subject — sports — and they have practiced their craft long enough to be at ease with the language. The best columnists are reporters who know how to use the language and are comfortable with words, Babcock said.

I have a tremendous regard for the English language. When a reporter sits down to write on deadline, the goal is to pound it out as quickly as you can. The most important thing is to get it done. When a sports writer covers a game, the first goal is to get the score and get it right.

OK, but I get perturbed when people are careless with the language. The writing is important; the grammar is important. When a columnist writes, there's no short deadline pressure, no excuse for not getting it right.

The position of staff columnist is a coveted one earned over time as a beat reporter. Media give columnists space on the page or on the air and time to write on topics of their choice, because their columns draw readers and viewers.

Opinion and commentary are clearly labeled to visually separate opinion from sports stories. Each has a column logo, a byline and usually a photo, also called a sig pic, of the writer. Some are set in different type or are justified ragged right to emphasize the difference in the content.

Functions

Columns entertain, educate, editorialize or comment. Some persuade, some inform, some encourage action or question ethics. Consumers today expect columns to make a point, Babcock said.

Online opinion options such as blogs, personal web pages and instant messaging have increased people's expectations that columnists will help them understand how to think about issues and people:

- Entertaining columns deliver their messages through humor or slice-of-life experiences. They help people look at life from the sidelines and laugh at themselves.
- Educational columns address issues: Should college athletes be paid? Should runners with prosthetic legs be allowed to participate in the Olympics? Is the current College Football Playoffs format working, or will the field eventually be expanded from four to eight? Or even more?
- Educational columns take an inside look, present facts or ideas as food for thought or explain the impact of an issue.
- Editorial columns express opinions, attempt to persuade, recommend an action or take a stand. Facts and quotations interpret and support the columnist's position.
- Brief comment columns are a collection of comments on unrelated topics. These crazy-quilt columns are often presented in a bulleted list.

Form

Although there is no set structure for columns, starting with an outline similar to that of a news story helps columnists organize what they want to say:

- Lead introduces the topic, usually an anecdote or delayed lead.
- Nut graf focuses the position of the column in one clear statement.
- Support uses facts, quotes, statistics and other material to explore the topic and support the position.
- Conclusion draws a conclusion from the data that restates the message, encourages an action and completes the set-up begun in the lead.

UPON FURTHER REVIEW

1. Find a sports story for each news value. Select one story that is news primarily because it is timely, one that is based on a conflict, one that is unusual, one about a prominent person, and so forth. Also, find one story in which all the news values are represented, and explain why you think it represents each. Which news values do most of the sports stories you read contain? Why do you think those values are the ones upon which news stories are most often based?

2. Choose three stories you think are written in inverted pyramid structure. In each, circle the paragraph you think is the nut graf. To see if a story is written in inverted pyramid, use the "cut" test. Starting at the bottom, cut off one paragraph at a time until you reach the point where the reader must have the information in that paragraph to know what the story is about (knows the 5 Ws). That paragraph should be the nut graf, and it may be the first paragraph if the story has a direct lead. If the story can be "cut" to the top two or three paragraphs, it's written in inverted pyramid structure.

3. Choose three online stories you think are written in Model T structure. Run the same cut test. A Model T story has paragraphs that might stand alone as "packages" of information, but each should be supplementary to the 5 Ws in the lead rather than integral to the understanding of what the story is about. A reader should know what the story is about, the 5 Ws, in the lead.

4. Find three sports stories you think are written in circular structure. Try the cut test on circular stories. What's the difference? What kinds of stories are written in circular structure: Gamers? Follow-ups? Profiles? Features? What news values do these stories represent?

5. If you were a columnist, what would your column say to readers? Would it entertain, educate, editorialize or comment? Describe the tone or persona your column would take, and choose a column head and tagline for it. Write four columns based on the selections you have chosen. Ask someone to read your columns and tell you what purpose and persona the columns seem to have. It takes practice to write a consistent column that readers look forward to reading, so keep writing and asking for feedback until you feel confident enough to submit samples to an editor.

ANSWERS TO THE CUT TEST
Right: Direct: can be cut to the first paragraph.
Left: Delayed: cannot be cut.

NOTES

1. Al Barkow, page 18 of "One Man's Mission," in the Jan. 18, 2008, issue of Golf World.

2. Drew Costley, "Nebraska volleyballer Pavan takes Honda-Broderick Cup," June 25, 2007, usatoday.com/sports/college/2007-06-25-pavan-honda_N.htm (accessed July 18, 2007).

3. Costley, "Nebraska volleyballer."

4. Ed Littler, KHAS-TV, 10 p.m. newscast, June 18, 2007.

5. Eric Olson, "NU's Pavan is female college athlete of the year," Associated Press, Hastings Tribune, June 26, 2007, 1C.

6. "Double amputee ruled eligible for Beijing," May 16, 2008, nbcsports.msnbc.com/id/24665015/ (accessed June 19, 2009).

7. Melvin Mencher, "News Reporting and Writing" (New York: McGraw-Hill, 2006), 99.

8. Associated Press, "Four Horsemen of Notre Dame." Reprinted by permission.

9. Eric Olson, "UC Irvine wins extra-inning thriller to eliminate Arizona State," Associated Press, Hastings Tribune, June 20, 2007, 1B.

10. Dirk Chatelain, "Spirit of the 70s," Omaha World-Herald, July 15, 2007, 1C.

11. Janet Kolodzy, "Convergence Journalism: Writing and Reporting across the News Media" (Lanham, MD: Rowman & Littlefield, 2006), 194.

12. "P.I.T. Crew racing toward top finish." Bronco 90 (Hastings, NE: Hastings College, 2005), 112.

13. Tim Harrower, "Inside Reporting: A Practical Guide to the Craft of Journalism" (New York: McGraw-Hill, 2007), 130.

14. Mike Babcock, freelance writer, personal interview, Jan. 15, 2008.

6

Following the Style

Readers like consistency.

More than half a century ago, the Associated Press created a stylebook because the news service organization recognized the need for a consistent style among stories from AP bureaus worldwide. Today, the Associated Press Stylebook is the standard in American journalism.[1]

It provides fundamental guidelines for spelling, language, usage, grammar, punctuation and journalistic style, and it supplies formats for information that appears frequently such as scores, times, distances, dates, addresses, names and titles.

AP STYLE

In media, the number of words a writer can use is limited by space on the page, seconds on the air and the attention span of the consumer online. Using a standardized style not only saves space and time, it makes writing easier and faster for reporters once they learn the guidelines. It makes grasping information easier and faster for readers who may not even realize a standard is being applied. It becomes a habit for the writer and a comfort zone for the consumer.

The Associated Press is committed to accuracy, clarity and conciseness in sports writing. The AP made guidelines that strive to be fair and not to offend any individual or group of people, according to Dr. Mike Sweeney, a journalism professor at Ohio University. The AP Stylebook also contains many entries intended to keep writers from making errors in fact, grammar and punctuation. It aims at "a general audience with a tone that is neither too elite nor too common," Sweeney said.[2]

While many writers and editors are most familiar with the printed AP Stylebook, AP also has an e-book edition and a digital AP Stylebook online, both searchable and portable, making it easy to access when a reporter is covering sporting events.

Most publications have in-house stylebooks in addition to the AP guidelines. Local stylebooks add rules for situations or preferences unique to that medium. The New

York Times, for instance, has such a complete set of guidelines that it publishes and sells its style manual.

Scores, times, distances, measurements — anything that recurs in news stories — are easier to read and understand if they appear in the same format every time. The date an event takes place, for example, might be written as a day of the week or as a date, depending upon the writer's habit, whim or mood. It could be written:

Sunday, January 17, 2048

Sunday, Jan. 17, 2048

Sunday, Jan. 17

Sunday

January 17

Jan. 17

Yesterday

Today

Tomorrow

Even more variations may be used for dates if the publication has weekly or monthly editions.

Using AP style, the date would be written:

Monday, Tuesday . . .	— within one week either way of publication
Jan. 17	— if the month is used with a day
Jan. 17	— if more than one week from date of publication but within the calendar year, omit the year
Jan. 17, 2048	— if outside the current calendar year, include the year
January 2048	— if used without a specific date, write out the month; do not separate with a comma

The words "yesterday," "today" and "tomorrow" make readers pause to calculate when the story appeared in relationship to today or tomorrow. If a story is delayed, such time references become inaccurate and require further editing before publication. Unless specified otherwise in the local newsroom's stylebook, use the day or the date.

Online sports news sites solve the problem of potential confusion by marking each story with the exact minute, hour and day of publication. Each time the story is updated, however, the time references within the story have to be adjusted accordingly, thus another reason for using the day of the week instead of yesterday, today or tomorrow.

Is Reggie Jackson "Mr. October," "Mister October" or "Mr. Oct."? Check the rules on courtesy titles, names and nicknames. Courtesy titles — Mr., Mrs., Miss or Ms. — are not commonly applied in sports, except in special situations such as Reggie "Mr. October" Jackson.

The style guide on names and nicknames is to write them the way the person prefers to be addressed. Nicknames, such as Laurence "Kool-Aid" Maroney, are always placed in quotation marks.

Numbers are all over the place in sports stories. So are the rules for writing them. In news style, single digit numbers are written as words, and double-digit and above numbers are written as numerals: one, nine, 10, 19, 119 — unless it's an exception, and there are many of those. When Mark Twain said, "Let the student beware the changes," he must have been contemplating numbers for sports stories.

Exceptions include ages, dates, heights, measurements, percents, proper names (Big Ten), scores, times, statistics and weights, which are always written in numerals whether they're single or double digits. The stylebook specifies the order in which scores and statistics are organized in stories and stats boxes and gives examples of the format.

The AP Stylebook has a separate sports style section. This section indicates how scores, times and distances should be written, defines sports terms and offers help with spelling and punctuating sports terms. (See Appendix A for examples from the AP Sports Guidelines and Style.)

Whether it's an editor, a sports reporter or the sports information or media relations director, anyone who writes for print or online media should know and use AP style. An editor or news director recognizes immediately whether the writer is a professional by the style used in a story or news release. Much less editing is required to prepare a story for release when it already conforms to AP style. That alone may make the difference in whether a story or news release is used or rejected by the journalist who reads it.

Broadcast sports departments also have stylebooks. Style will change when the reporter is writing for listeners who only have one chance to hear and understand the information. Because broadcast stories are shorter, it is even more important to omit extraneous words that take up airtime that could be used to report significant information.

HEADLINES

The Chicago Bulls were preparing to play the Utah Jazz for the NBA Championship. It would be the Bulls' sixth championship in eight years if they won. Amid the tension and excitement, the Chicago Tribune was preparing for the front page that would run the morning after the championship game. Win or lose, readers would expect a big headline.

Bill Parker, then assistant managing editor, canvassed the newspaper's headline writers and gathered a list of ideas about what the headline should incorporate. He knew he had space for four to six words at the top of the front page to capture the spirit of a sports-crazed city.

The Bulls won 87-86 on a steal and shot in the last five seconds. The streets of Chicago "erupted in an all-night celebration," according to James Glen Stovall in "The Complete Editor,"[3] and waited for the Tribune's morning headline which "summed up the feelings of the Bulls fans at the moment with a wink toward another type of physical activity" and an allusion to a popular New York Times best-seller: "The Joy of Sex." The sixth championship for the Bulls was, indeed,

The joy of six

Headlines Sell Benefits

Headlines are ads that sell stories to potential readers by promising a benefit for reading the story. That little "wink" of an allusion to the famous book by almost the same name implies the benefits of happiness, humor and satisfaction for the reader who reads on.

Some readers are looking for stories they expect to be there: last night's big game, who made the cut for the next round of the playoffs or which team is favored to win the Super Bowl. Some readers are in the market for any story about favorite teams or players. Some readers are just grazing, looking for a good story to read.

Each decides whether to read the story based on the headline. Information, entertainment, mystery and amusement are among the benefits a headline may offer as a value for time spent reading.

The popularity of online news sites has made headlines even more critical in getting readers' attention and drawing them into the story. The Poynter Institute conducts Eyetrack studies using sophisticated technology to follow the eye movements of print and online news readers to find out, among other things, whether readers were attracted first by the headlines, the photos or something else.[4]

The first Eyetrack studies showed that online readers noticed and scanned headlines first.[5] They checked out the first two or three words of a headline or text block before making a decision to read on or leave. The majority of online readers in the most recent study tended to enter at the upper left of a screen and settle on a dominant element, most often a photograph, first. Faces in photos and videos attracted the most attention.

Print readers looked first at headlines and then at large photos. Even on smartphones, readers follow the traditional upper left to lower right pattern when looking at a screen.

All of the major readability studies conclude that, above all, content is king. If a sports fan is looking for the story about his or her favorite team, that is where that person's eyes will stop first even if it's necessary to scan more than one page or screen to find it.

Writing Headlines

Names appear to be the secret to writing sports headlines. Names of teams. Names of mascots. Names of players and coaches. An informal survey of sports stories in newspapers and on sports web sites showed more than 90 percent of the headlines begin with the name of a team, a mascot, a player or a coach.

Typically, headlines are written by copy editors or page designers during the pagination or uploading process and not by the reporter who wrote the story. Newsletter editors, news release writers and promotions designers usually write their own headlines.

Headline writers have the task of reducing each story to a few words that will fit in the space left above the text when the page is designed. A one-column story will accommodate one or at most two very small words per line — and present one very big challenge for the headline writer. Columnist Mike Sweeney wrote in the Fort Worth Star-Telegram:

> "Names like Moe Iba fit well in headlines and are appreciated by copy editors. When Iba was an assistant coach at the University . . . the college newspaper ran a story saying he had turned down a job elsewhere. An editor who drew the page called for a headline so tight that only three little words would fit, and 'Iba rejects job' was too long."[6]

The solution was:

Moe no go

Or take this one-column, tongue-in-cheek commentary on the Miss America Pageant dropping the 96-year-old tradition of a parade of young ladies in bathing suits:

Swimsuit
contest being
put out to dry

TIPS FOR WRITING HEADLINES

- Represent the story accurately.

- Use specific, concise words.

- Use conversational language.

  This: *Four Horsemen of Notre Dame trot across goal line*

  Not: *Quad of equestrians flay flanks in battle for pigskin*

- Use present tense for past and present events.

  This: *UNC crunches Mental State in Popcorn Bowl*

  Not: *UNC crunched Mental State in Popcorn Bowl*

- Use action verbs.

  This: *Yeager earns new position*

  Not: *Yeager has new position*

- Replace "a," "an" and "the" with information.

  This: *Olympian carries torch, lights flame*

  Not: *An Olympic runner carries the torch*

- Replace "and" with a comma in lists.

  This: *Kenyan, Australian qualify for semifinals*

  Not: *Kenyan and Australian qualify for semifinals*

- Do not split subject-verb, preposition-object, modifier-noun.

  This: *Dottseon wants fans*
          with team in bowl momentum

  Not: *Dottseon wants fans with*
          team in bowl momentum

  This: *Baseball commission adopts*
          new policy to control drug use

  Not: *Baseball commission adopts new*
          policy to control drug use

- Avoid double meanings.

  This: *Commission gets complaints about NBA officials*

  Not: *Complaints about NBA officials growing ugly*

- Omit "to be" verbs.

  This: *Summer Olympics headed to China*

  Not: *Olympic games are headed to China*

- Use infinitive form of verb for future tense.

  This: *Boerigter to receive Hall of Fame honor*

  Not: *Boerigter will receive Hall of Fame honor*

- Fit space.

  Headline should fill at least 90 percent of allowed space.

- Read aloud.

  Emphasize a different word each time to hear rhythm, double meanings, bad splits, awkward phrasing.

Most headlines have the luxury of room for four to six words, maybe more if there is space for more than one line. In those few words, the writer is challenged to summarize the story in such a way that it is specific and accurate while selling the story to the reader and not misrepresenting the reporter's work or distorting the meaning of the story.

The sentence, or down style, headline is the most common style. The first word is always capitalized, but no end punctuation mark is necessary. A sentence headline uses the English rules of capitalization, contains a subject and a verb, and conveys a complete thought.

Huskies hammer Arizona State

Knights trample King's men

Rain washes out Cup practice, jumbles schedule

Headlines omit articles (a, an, the), conjunctions (and, but, or) and most adjectives and adverbs. Articles and conjunctions may be used if needed to help make a headline fit, but they're always optional. Question marks and exclamation points are the only terminal punctuation used. Those are rare, but they do make the headlines on special occasions.

A question mark in this headline wonders of Notre Dame:

Will Irish eyes smile this spring?

Another uncertainty led to this Idaho Statesman headline:[7]

Pacman Jones getting ready to . . . wrestle?

This special-section label headline in the Honolulu Star-Advertiser celebrated the University of Hawaii's come-from-behind win over Washington for a chance at the national playoffs:[8]

Perfect!

'Perfect!' timing and a lot of hustle

AFTER DEADLINE
By Mark Platte

The Advertiser's special four-page edition with the headline "Perfect!" made it onto ESPN and local television stations just seconds after the Warriors' come-from-behind victory against Washington.

The idea of a front page printed in advance and handed out right after the game is not new, but to do it right and get it on the field in front of the cameras requires a lot of luck and perfect timing.

We printed 16,000 copies of the section on the morning of Saturday's game and kept them under wraps in two Advertiser vans until the end of the game. When it was 21-0 Washington after the first quarter, it looked like our time and effort had been wasted. But by halftime, the Warriors had managed to stay within a touchdown of the lead.

With 10 minutes left in the game, Lester Kodama, our single-copy manager, called together his crew of about 40 teenagers who usually hand out our Bowtime football programs and hid the papers in garbage bags. The teens remained outside the gates to hand the papers to departing fans while Kodama went inside with a bundle of 300 papers.

Only two minutes remained when I called Kodama from the sidelines. When I got his voice-mail, I started to get nervous. It was important that the papers get into the hands of players just as the game ended so they could get maximum exposure.

With 44 seconds left, Colt Brennan connected with Ryan Grice-Mullins for the lead, and I connected with Kodama. But with the stadium roaring, we had a hard time hearing each other as we tried to arrange a meeting spot. I was at the 10-yard line on the mauka side, and I needed Kodama to meet me at the 20-yard line. Just then, I saw Alvin Katahara, our market development director, and Jay Higa, our classified advertising director, arrive and ready to help.

Kodama appeared from the stands just in time, and we raced toward him, tearing into the bundle. Fans were eager to get copies, and someone grabbed four from the stack. But by the time we turned to the field, Washington had a first down at the Hawai'i 4-yard line. It appeared the Huskies were going to tie the game, and Kodama grabbed two of the papers back. The other two made their first appearance on national television.

We hid 200 papers as best we could while praying Washington would not tie the game. Ryan Mouton's interception with three seconds remaining had everyone swarming the field, and the pages felt safe to hand out. I approached coach June Jones with a copy but he was hustling everyone off the field because there was still time to play.

Mayor Mufi Hannemann got the first copy and UH athletic director Herman Frazier got the second. Then the players and coaches got the next batch. The players must have thought we literally printed the paper on the spot, judging from their puzzled looks.

Kodama was mobbed in the stands as he passed out about 100 papers. Then he got word back to the teens to break open the garbage bags and man the gates

for the cheering fans leaving the game. Katahara, Higa and I remained on the field as players started mugging for the cameras and holding the pages aloft.

But there were 1,000 papers left that Katahara smartly held back for the next day's rally at the Stan Sheriff Center.

Five minutes after the gates were open that Sunday, the papers were gone. Only a few precious copies remain in our possession.

"It was good to see the fans were so passionate about UH and what the team has done," Katahara said. "They were hungry for something that was a souvenir of a memorable season."

Mark Platte is senior vice president/editor of The Honolulu Advertiser. Reach him at mplatte@honoluluadvertiser.com or 525-8080. Or post your comments at honoluluadvertiser.com.

PHOTO 6.1

Perfect! timing and a lot of hustle.

"PERFECT!" TIMING AND A LOT OF HUSTLE

The Advertiser's special four-page edition with the headline "Perfect!" made it onto ESPN and local television stations just seconds after the Warriors' come-from-behind victory against Washington.

The idea of a front page printed in advance and handed out right after the game is not new, but to do it right and get it on the field in front of the cameras requires a lot of luck and perfect timing.

We printed 16,000 copies of the section on the morning of Saturday's game and kept them under wraps in two Advertiser vans until the end of the game. When it was 21-0 Washington after the first quarter, it looked like our time and effort had been wasted. But by halftime, the Warriors had managed to stay within a touchdown of the lead.

With 10 minutes left in the game, Lester Kodama, our single-copy manager, called together his crew of about 40 teenagers who usually hand out our Bowtime football programs and hid the papers in garbage bags. The teens remained outside the gates to hand the papers to departing fans while Kodama went inside with a bundle of 300 papers.

Only two minutes remained when I called Kodama from the sidelines. When I got his voicemail, I started to get nervous. It was important that the papers get into the hands of players just as the game ended so they could get maximum exposure.

With 44 seconds left, Colt Brennan connected with Ryan Grice-Mullins for the lead, and I connected with Kodama. But with the stadium roaring, we had a hard time hearing each other as we tried to arrange a meeting spot. I was at the 10-yard line on the mauka side, and I needed Kodama to meet me at the 20-yard line. Just then, I saw Alvin Katahara, our market development director, and Jay Higa, our classified advertising director, arrive ready to help.

Kodama appeared from the stands just in time, and we raced toward him, tearing into the bundle. Fans were eager to get copies, and someone grabbed four from the stack. But by the time we turned to the field, Washington had a first down at the Hawai'i 4-yard line. It appeared the Huskies were going to tie the game, and Kodama grabbed two of the papers back. The other two made their first appearance on national television.

We hid 200 papers as best we could while praying Washington would not tie the game. Ryan Mouton's interception with three seconds remaining had everyone swarming the field, and the pages felt safe to hand out. I approached coach June Jones with a copy, but he was hustling everyone off the field because there was still time to play.

Mayor Mufi Hannemann got the first copy and UH athletic director Herman Frazier got the second. Then the players and coaches got the next batch. The players must have thought we literally printed the paper on the spot, judging from their puzzled looks.

Kodama was mobbed in the stands as he passed out about 100 papers. Then he got word back to the teens to break open the garbage bags and man the gates for the cheering fans leaving the game. Katahara, Higa and I remained on the field as players started mugging for the cameras and holding the pages aloft.

But there were 1,000 papers left that Katahara smartly held back for the next day's rally at the Stan Sheriff Center.

Five minutes after the gates were open that Sunday, the papers were gone. Only a few precious copies remain in our possession.

"It was good to see the fans were so passionate about UH and what the team has done," Katahara said. "They were hungry for something that was a souvenir of a memorable season."

— Reprinted with permission from the Honolulu Star-Advertiser

Action Verbs

Action verbs are the lifeblood of sports headlines. "McIlroy takes lead" or "McIlroy leads" would state the fact, but "McIlroy grabs lead" gives a stronger sense of the intensity and momentum.

When choosing an action verb, make the action it implies appropriate for the subject in the situation. A horse in the final leg of the race gallops to the finish line, but a soccer player does not gallop to the goal. A baseball player slides home, but a basketball player does not slide to the bucket.

Cats can pounce, and a player can be jazzed if he's just been traded to the Utah Jazz.

Wildcats pounce on depleted Tigers

Korver's Jazzed, joins team on the road

USING PUNCTUATION IN HEADLINES

- Use only when necessary to understanding.
- Use comma to replace "and."

  Patriots, Giants play for season record

  Gill, Cotton candidates for coaching staff

- Use colon to indicate the source said this, usually paraphrased.

  Frost: do nothing before last game

- Use single quotes to indicate source's words.

  Bunner: 'A minute left. You can do it'

  Coach calls game 'perfect'

- Use question marks, exclamation points.

  Bye, Bill?

- Use numerals, decimals, $.

  $1.5M most ever for rookie

- Use capital letters for races and money.

  Brooks wins 10K, collects $5K

Secondary Headlines

Secondary headlines add layers of information between the headline and the text. They serve two quite opposite purposes: to encourage readers to read the rest of the story and to give readers enough information to know some facts about the story if they decide not to read more.

Secondary headlines are set in type smaller than the headline and larger than the text. They may be longer phrases or complete sentences that convey additional facts and details. More than one may be used with a story.

Deuel swings ahead, Jennings misses cut
Senior Haydo Wall sinks 4-footer on 14th
in Saturday's Iron Horse Classic

Sodbusters prepared to make history

The Sodbusters will travel to face
the Prairie Wolves in their
final battle for a perfect season.
Taking the Conference lead
after besting the Wolves 77-76
in their last match at home,
the Sodbusters are raring to go.

Punctuation and Style

Headline syntax and punctuation differ from standard English grammar rules because of space limitations. Periods are not used, commas replace "and" and a colon connects a speaker's name and message.

Seattle stymies Washington's rally, wins in NFC playoffs

Lenson recovers to win sprint finish, Dawson leads overall

Richardson: Landis fills stat sheet all the way across

Single quotation marks replace double quotation marks around words quoted in the story.

'Once-in-a-lifetime' shot sends Bradley to top

Texas QB 'ready to go' for KC

Cicotello chasing 'Hawai'i Slam'

The dollar sign is the only symbol used in text, but symbols such as &, @, # and % appear in headlines as space-saving devices or for graphic illustration of a subject.

¢ turn into $ for baseball retirees' fund

Martini to earn $1.1M first year

Numbers may be written as words or numerals.

#1 or not, Pepperdine has best finish

Woe and 2 for the Pacers

Six car crash slows Indy 500

Coach has five-year deal

CHECKLIST FOR HEADLINES

☐ Is it accurate?

☐ Is it a complete thought?

☐ Does it sound conversational?

☐ Does it use active voice?

    This: Ruth bats in three

    Not: Three batted in by Ruth

☐ Does it have an action verb?

☐ Does the punctuation further understanding?

☐ Can "a," "an," "the," or "and" be replaced by more informative words?

☐ Are grammatical constructions on the same line?

    subject and verb

    preposition and object

    noun and modifier

☐ Does it fit without altering publication font or size style?

☐ Are the largest headlines at the top of the page?

Blurbs and Links

Blurbs (also called intro headlines or talk heads) are the online equivalent of secondary headlines. Like secondary headlines in print, blurbs tell online readers what's in the news and help them decide what stories to read. More than one blurb may appear with a story or brief.

Eyetrack research showed that half of online readers are scanners who move quickly from one headline or blurb to another, seldom returning to read a story once they move away from it. By scanning the visual chunks created by headlines and blurbs, these readers gain an overview of the news.

Links connect online readers with even more layers of information and access options. Online stories have the added advantage of being able to use embedded links to lead readers to sites about related topics and give them more choices in selecting the information they want. An online reader may never finish reading a news story yet have a more thorough understanding of the event or subject than someone who reads the whole story, because of the ability to follow the thread of information from link to link through more sources.

An online reader who wants to know more about that NBA championship game might link to the NBA Encyclopedia Playoff Edition to read a retrospective story about the game, to YouTube to watch video of the final shot, to Amazon to buy a book or the video "Unforgettabulls" from the NBA Championship Series, or to the New York Times archives for stories published about the game.

CAPTIONS

Today's news is tomorrow's history. Even if most people would recognize the person in the photo today, a researcher would be unable to track the photo without names and details for identification. The significance of the event would be lost if the caption did not provide the name or names of those pictured, the location and the occasion.

"Caption" and "cutline" are interchangeable terms meaning the words that describe what's happening in a photo. Before photography and printing press technology converged in the 1800s, the only way to get an illustration in the newspaper was to carve or "cut" the image into a wood block that could be inserted alongside the type on the printing plate. Images became known as "cuts," and the name has stuck through all the technological advances in photography and printing.

Every photograph, including a mugshot, needs a caption. Whether it's online, on a page in a newspaper or magazine or in a company newsletter, a photograph is just a graphic design element unless it's accompanied by a caption explaining who is in the photo, what is happening, when and where it took place and why it's newsworthy. The sports editor may know by looking at a photo that it's quarterback Tom Brady sweating out the last few minutes of the game that gave the New England Patriots a 16-0 season, but do not assume everyone who sees the photo will have the same instant recognition.

Captions identify the people in the photo. As a general guideline, journalists go by the "rule of five": if up to five persons are recognizable in a photograph, and they are all involved in the action, each should be identified by name. In a shot of four players sitting on the bench with their heads down as the opponent makes the winning point that knocks them out of the playoffs, each should be named.

If the coach is pictured standing on the sideline shaking his fist at the officials, and four players on the bench behind him are identifiable, only the coach needs to be identified because he is the center of the action. The bench provides background that establishes the environment in which the action is taking place. The players are just part of that environment. It would not be wrong to name them, but it is not necessary.

This "rule of five" is flexible. If six or seven people wearing hard hats and holding shovels poised to break ground for the new stadium are pictured, they should all be

PHOTO 6.2
Photographers are part of the news production team. They take and select photos and write captions.
iStock Essentials/Scyther5.

named. If two or three players are shown making a key play and faces in the crowd behind them could be identified, only the players need to be named.

Photographers are responsible for gathering the information about the photographs they take, including the correct spelling of names, and filing it with the photographs for future reference.

Captions should also tell readers what they cannot see by looking at the photograph. For instance, if the photo is of a groundbreaking ceremony for a new athletic complex, the reader wants to know why these particular people are breaking the ground, how much construction is going to cost and whether it will be ready in time for next season.

Avoid grip-and-grin handshakes and posed photos, even if that is the CEO of an athletic shoe manufacturing company presenting a multimillion-dollar check to a local university. The caption can explain in great detail the significance of that handshake, but readers will probably not stop to read it. Staged or studio photos, including mugshots, draw relatively little attention from readers, according to the Eyetrack study.

Posed team photos appear in special preseason sections and on posters. Every player, coach and team assistant is named in the caption. The in-house stylebook defines when

CHECKLIST FOR CAPTIONS

☐ Identifies who, what, where, when and why

☐ Names key people in photo

☐ Explains significance of event

☐ Captures action in present tense

☐ Avoids clichés such as looks on, poses with, is pictured, struts stuff, while (name) looks on

☐ Confirms:

- Number of names in caption matches number of principal persons in photo.
- Names matched to faces.
- Names spelled correctly.
- Identities checked again.

and how team photos are published and how the caption will be written: first initial and last name, first and last names, last name comma first initial or another way.

Captions can be as long as necessary to make the photo understandable without stating the obvious. "Coach Big Shot poses in his office" is easy to see from looking at the photo, but the reader wants to know more: Why is the coach in his office? What's newsworthy about this photo? "Coach Big Shot prepares to watch films and take notes for next week's game before meeting with the team Sunday evening" explains why the coach is taking notes as he watches the screen on the corner of his desk.

Photos capture the action as it is happening. Captions describe the action as though it were happening at the present time, in present tense. "Coach Big Shot watches . . . and takes . . ." says he is doing it as the reader watches. The next sentence or sentences may be past tense if they explain the background leading up to this moment.

LIBEL AND OTHER LEGALITIES

Sports writers are subject to the same laws as all journalists when it comes to saying or writing words that are untrue or harmful to others. Writers are responsible for knowing and abiding by federal and state laws and the codes of ethics of their profession.

A commitment to accuracy is the best protection a journalist can have. Failure to check facts, or the inability to support those facts, is the cause of most libel suits. At the very least, publishing an incorrectly spelled player's name or the wrong score damages the credibility of the reporter and the publication. At most, reporters lose jobs and courts order millions of dollars paid to persons who have been libeled or whose privacy has been invaded.

Here is a brief overview of the legal terms sports writers should know.

Libel

Libel is printed defamation of character, an untruth that damages a person's reputation or hinders that person's possibility of getting or holding a job. The statement must be untrue and be about an identifiable person to be grounds for libel.

A generalization such as "golfers are crooks" is not libelous because it does not identify an individual. "Dick Krapff is a crook" would be libelous if it damages Krapff's reputation as golf cart manager at the local country club or keeps him from getting another job. If Krapff sold used golf carts from the course and pocketed the money, he might be a crook. But until or unless he is charged with stealing from his employer, it would be libelous to say so.

Newspapers, magazines, emails, tweets, websites and broadcast scripts are considered sources of print text. Live, unscripted broadcasts that are preserved in a tangible form such as video, podcast or digital recordings are also subject to allegations of libel.

Slander is spoken defamation of character and is subject to the same laws as libel. If based on unscripted speech, however, slander is treated as a lesser offense because its effects are less permanent. A script or a recording of the speech would constitute publication, making the charge libel. One defense for libel is truth. The information must be provable and not used with wrongful intentions or ill will, especially as increasing guilt of certain offenses. If the printed information can be proven, through documentation or court record, it is a statement of fact and not libel. Most questions of libel are the result of the reporter's negligence. Always verify information before using it. False information reported as fact, even if used as a quotation and attributed to the source, is libelous and is the reporter's responsibility.

Use of the word "alleged" and not identifying a person by name are not defenses against libel. If the number of persons to whom the libelous information might apply is small enough that one or all of the individuals feel they could be singled out as the injured party, say, members of a college tennis or softball team, each may file charges.

Public Figures and Private Persons

Public figures are persons who have voluntarily put themselves in the public eye in such a way that they gain prominence, fame or notoriety. By virtue of their voluntary and intentional action to earn a living through an activity that is supported by the public, professional athletes and coaches, like entertainers, are considered to be public figures.

Access to media has traditionally been considered a factor in determining who is a public figure. A person who has regular and open access to the media through news conferences with reporters, or one whom the media seeks out to interview because of the person's newsworthiness, is likely to be considered a public figure. This definition may be expanding since Twitter essentially gives everyone access to the media today.

For a public figure to bring a libel charge against a reporter or the media, that person would have to prove the information was false and that the media publishing the material knew it was false before it was published. If that is true, the reporter or media acted with intent to create ill will toward, or to intentionally defame, the public figure.

Private figures, persons who are not paid to perform their roles as athletes or coaches, have more protection under the law than do public figures, according to the Supreme Court. Most high school, college and amateur athletes do not have to prove cause when they believe they have been libeled. Negligence, which usually results from carelessness on the reporter's part, is cause enough for the court to acknowledge libel on the part of a private person.

Corrections

Mistakes happen, and they should be corrected as quickly, publicly and honestly as possible. Truth, and the fact that the error is acknowledged quickly and without prompting, is often enough to calm the injured person and prevent a libel suit. A show of good faith on the reporter's part does not undo the damage done to someone's reputation, but it may be looked upon favorably in court.

Privilege and Fair Comment

Journalists are protected in expressing opinions, even if the comments are negative or critical, by privilege. Privilege covers the right of a journalist to report information and statements made in official governmental proceedings, such as courts, without fear of being sued even if the information is false or the statements would be libelous in another context.

Privilege also protects journalists' right to express opinion. It does not protect inaccurate or false information masquerading as opinion. A columnist who writes that a coach made a stupid decision at a critical point in the game or that an official made a bad call that caused a team to lose a key game is protected by privilege because those are opinions and the topic of many a postgame debate. If, however, a columnist says the coach is stupid because he bribed players, that columnist is not protected by privilege and had better have proof to show that, in fact, cash and cars were made available to players.

Fair comment allows journalists to publish columns and editorials commenting on professional players, coaches and athletic directors for things they do, directly or indirectly, if the action is a matter of public interest. When a coach at a state university gets a big raise paid for with tax dollars or a prominent athlete attacks a woman walking her dog along a residential street and leaves her unconscious and bleeding, it's a matter of interest to the public's pocketbooks and personal safety.

In turn, the journalist's obligation is to write commentary and analysis that is factually accurate.

Open Records and Open Meetings Laws

Sports reporters occasionally have reason to attend a court session where an athlete is being arraigned or sentenced. They may need to see the police report on a traffic violation or an accident to gather or verify information.

Each state has sunshine laws, so called because they allow the "sun to shine in" on public records, public meetings and court proceedings. Laws vary from state to state, but almost all court proceedings and court records are open to the public. It's a matter of finding them. Some traffic violations and accident reports may be on file at the courthouse and others at the police station, firehouse or city hall.

Not every public official or government agency is willing to hand out information on a moment's notice, so plan ahead. Know where the information is located and get acquainted with the people in the offices.

Even a sports reporter can benefit from reading the state and local statutes. A tour of local public offices will make finding the right place and the right information much faster when a deadline looms and the only way to get the official information is to look at the original document.

More public records are available online every day, but be aware that the websites containing them may not be up-to-date or fully archived.

THE FAIR USE QUESTION

"Fair use" is a legal doctrine that allows individuals, and sometimes business entities such as media producers, to use copyright-protected material under carefully controlled circumstances without getting permission from the copyright owner. In this book, for instance, the Associated Press owns the copyright to the photo of the "Four Horsemen of Notre Dame" and to the AP Sports Guidelines and Style in appendix A. They have been reprinted by permission of the Associated Press. Owners of copyrighted works such as these may, at their discretion, charge a fee for the use of their property.

Courts interpret fair use on the merits of individual cases and the history of previous decisions. Overall, it is the courts that determine current guidelines applying to sports media, basing rulings on those violation of copyright factors listed in the previous section.

No definitive rules exist to determine how much of any copyrighted work is allowed to be used without permission — so when in doubt, ask. Examples of acceptable fair use would likely include

- A few lines of a song or excerpts from a book in a review.
- A drawing of a copyrighted cartoon character in a staff-drawn editorial cartoon in a student publication.
- A limited amount of copyrighted material in a parody.
- News video in which copyrighted music provides ambient sound at a newsworthy event.
- Up to one minute of copyrighted audio or video in a news setting, such as an obituary of a famed athlete.

Writers and creators of music, videos, films, sports documentaries, podcasts, DVDs, graphics, electronic messages and the like should never assume that giving a credit line or a disclaimer to the source of copyrighted material will allow them to claim fair use. Adding your own work to an already copyrighted work does not make it fair use. More leniency may be allowed in work created for entertainment or nonprofit purposes such as parodies, mash-ups and remixes, but there's no legal guarantee.

© COPYRIGHT

Copyright is a symbol. Copyright is a law. Copyright is an attempt to keep people from stealing the work others have created and claiming it as their own, usually for profit. For journalists, presenting accurate information in a news story is the main reason for wanting to use the work of others. Law allows the use of limited amounts of copyrighted work in news contexts. However, if a journalist used the same material in a book without securing permission, that would be a violation of copyright.

Copyright protects any creative work in a tangible form including written words, art, photographs, music, video, film and online works such as podcasts and blogs. From the moment an idea is put into words or on canvas or recorded digitally or sent in an electronic message, the creation is copyrighted. Depending upon the date the work was created, it may be legally protected for 100 years or more. The law establishes copyright as the life of the author plus 70 years.

All the work done by someone employed to write or produce material, such as photos or video, is known as work-made-for-hire. A sports reporter employed by a newspaper, broadcast station or website, for instance, does not own the copyright on work done for the medium; the employer owns the right to the work. The copyright on work-made-for-hire is 95 years.

It's safest to assume that any quotation, graphic, photo or recording a sports writer might want to use is copyright protected and permission is needed to use it in any new way. However, the law permits a few exceptions. In addition to news reporting, the law allows limited use of copyrighted work for purposes such as criticism, comment, teaching, scholarship or research without infringing on the owner's copyright.

Determination of a violation of copyright will be decided by the court based upon

- The intended character and use (commercial, educational, news reporting).
- The nature of the copyrighted work.
- The portion of the work used in relation to the work as a whole.
- The effect of the use on the potential value of the original work.

Both the words Super Bowl and the logo are copyright-protected trademarks. The name Super Bowl, for example, may be used in a story without permission as long as it is written as two words, each capitalized (AP style). The trademarked Super Bowl logo may also be used in editorial copy such as a feature page or an infographic, with the proper trademark symbol, but it may not be reprinted in any commercial or promotional context without securing written permission and paying licensing fees. A sports bar advertising a special event on the day of the Super Bowl must call it "The Big Game Day Bash" or the "Game of the Year Gathering," rather than "Super Bowl Extravaganza." This guideline would apply to Super Bowl podcasts, YouTube videos and other electronically published material.

The same principle applies to all trademarks whether they are the names of companies such as Nike and Adidas or the names and logos of schools.

Securing written permission from the owner is the fair and safe way to use any copyright-protected work. Finding the current owner of a copyright may not be easy. Copyrights are sometimes sold with the work, or the owner may have died, making it difficult to find the family members who own it. If the request is to use the material for personal profit or commercial use, expect to pay to use it. And be aware that the process itself takes time.

Commercial Use

Use of copyrighted material in an advertisement or promotion without written permission is a violation of copyright. This includes words, photos, trademarks, logos and graphics.

The use of photos and endorsements in commercial advertising requires the signed consent of the person or persons pictured or named. The use of an athlete's photo to promote a product without that person's consent would be unlawful. The easiest way to avoid a commercial use suit is to have signed permission forms on file for everyone in any photo that could potentially be used in advertising or promotion, including promotion of the school student-athletes attend.

Online Media Issues

Internet users are still exploring the frontiers of media and communication law. Online discussion groups, blogs and citizen journalist websites were of concern to internet service providers until the Supreme Court ruled that service providers are not responsible for messages posted by users. Thus media websites that encourage public participation in blogs and instant messaging cannot be held responsible for comments posted by users.

Libel, copyright and commercial use laws applying to print and broadcast media apply equally to online media whether the source is a company website, a Facebook page or a personal email, according to James Tidwell, a copyright expert who taught journalism at Eastern Illinois University.

Reporters who record interviews for rebroadcast at a later time, or broadcast telephone conversations live without the knowledge of the person speaking, open themselves up to libel and invasion of privacy charges. Consent laws determine whether the state is a one-party consent state, in which a conversation may be recorded without the knowledge of both parties, or a two-person consent state, in which both parties must be aware that the conversation is being recorded.

A general rule of operation is to document all calls by recording acknowledgment and permission from the person being called before beginning an interview or live broadcast. Call-in shows are an exception. Participants call with the intention of speaking live on the air and are personally responsible for what they say.

CODE OF ETHICS

Although no industrywide code of ethics exists for journalists, most newsrooms have ethics guidelines in their policies or stylebooks. The Associated Press Sports Editors has adopted such guidelines specifically for sports journalists. In principle, the APSE guidelines address the issues and situations that might compromise the integrity and obligation of reporters and editors to produce fair and unbiased sports news, including, but not limited to, those in the box on page 115.

Media relations writers, freelancers and sports information directors whose employers do not have stated ethics policies may choose to adopt the Society of Professional Journalists' Code of Ethics as a standard for all communications with the media and the public.

For a sports writer, these guidelines mean being extra careful to represent both teams equally in a story even though you're a homer at heart; making just one more call after trying all day to reach a player and give her the chance to defend herself against allega-

APSE GUIDELINES

Journalists maintain professionalism by not:

- Accepting tickets, travel, gifts and gratuities.

  The media source should pay travel and meal expenses for staff, even when they travel on a charter flight or dine with a team they are covering. Gifts of more than token value should be declined, returned or given to charity.

- Participating in athletic events, including serving as an official stats or scorekeeper.

  Writers should avoid involvement with outside activities that could be viewed as a conflict of interest, including serving as a scorekeeper for a team they may at some time be assigned to cover.

- Using credentials and press box communications equipment.

  The media source should pay for the use of on-site communications equipment at events, and, outside of established reciprocal relationships, for tickets and press credentials for staff members.

- Endorsing commercial trade names and sponsorships.

  In editorial matter, avoid using product names or endorsements except where necessary to properly identify an event.

- Accepting outside employment.

  Reporters should not accept outside employment that would create a conflict, or the perception of a conflict, in the publication's coverage

  — Adapted from Associated Press Sports Editors Ethical Guidelines[9]

tions of steroid use before the story goes to press; and encouraging the public to express their opinions to and about the media openly via email, tweet, blog or call.

It means not accepting tickets, meals or gifts that might obligate you to someone who expects a favor in return; not putting yourself in situations that might be perceived as a show of support for one team over another; not marching in that protest demonstration even though you strongly agree with the sentiment; and not giving in to the temptation to make a couple of calls to get enough information to write your story because you'd just really rather stay home than travel to the game.

It means treating sources, colleagues and the public with respect and admitting to and correcting mistakes when you're wrong.

SPJ CODE OF ETHICS

- Seek truth and report it.

    Journalists should be honest, fair and courageous in gathering, reporting and interpreting information.

- Minimize harm.

    Ethical journalists treat sources, subjects and colleagues as human beings deserving of respect.

- Act independently.

    Journalists should be free of obligation to any interest other than the public's right to know.

- Be accountable.

    Journalists are accountable to their readers, listeners, viewers and each other.

—Adapted from the Society of Professional Journalists' Code of Ethics[10]

UPON FURTHER REVIEW

1. Read the examples from the AP Sports Guidelines and Style in Appendix A. Compare sports stories in a newspaper or on an online sports news site with the AP guidelines. Try to find examples of these guidelines. What exceptions did you find? Look at several stories to see if the same guideline is applied in all stories and publications. Why do you think the source uses a different style for any exceptions? Note: The AP Stylebook publishes a new edition annually, so some variations may be because AP has adapted to current usage.

2. Ask for a copy of a local media style guide (each newsroom has its own style rules in addition to AP). Ask the reporter or news director to explain why the newsroom formulated the specific guidelines in its book. If your office or newsroom does not have a style guide, make a list of guidelines you would want to have included and ask others to contribute ideas. Discuss the suggestions with your colleagues, classmates or employer. Draft a style guide and add to it as you find yourself questioning the way in which something should be written.

3. Study the headlines on sports stories in five sources. What similarities do you notice among the sources? Differences? Make a list of the most descriptive action verbs and figure the percentage compared to those with understood or nondescriptive verbs. Rewrite some of the not-so-interesting headlines using higher interest verbs. Count the number of headlines that begin with the name of a team, mascot, player or coach and calculate the percent. Compare to the percent on news pages. Is there a difference? Why?

4. As a sports reporter, what would you want to have included in a code of ethics for sports journalists? Should it be different from a code for all journalists? Explain your rationale. If your office does not have a code of ethics, or it has one that has not been reviewed recently, draft a list of topics that might be included and circulate it among your colleagues for their input. As a team, discuss the need for a formal code and the suggestions for what it should include. Draft or update a code for your workplace.

NOTES

1. Norm Goldstein, ed., "Associated Press Stylebook and Briefing on Media Law" (New York: Associated Press, 2007).

2. Michael Sweeney, "The guide to AP style," Aug. 27, 2007, http://web.archive.org/web/20071024002142/www.usu.edu/journalism/faculty/sweeney/re (accessed June 19, 2009).

3. James Glen Stovall and Edward Mullins, "The Complete Editor" (Boston: Allyn and Bacon, 2006), 134.

4. Sara Quinn, "Eyetrack07 ASNE presentation script," March 28, 2007, poynter.org/content/content_print.asp?id=120470&custom= (accessed Jan. 12, 2008).

5. Nora Paul and Laura Ruel, "Early lessons from Poynter's Eyetrack07," April 14, 2007, ojr.org/ojr/stories/070414paul/print.htm (accessed Jan. 13, 2008).

6. Sweeney, http://web.archive.org/web/20071024002142/www.usu.edu/journalism/faculty/sweeney/re.

7. "Pacman Jones is getting ready to . . . wrestle?" Idaho Statesman, Aug. 7, 2007, 3 (Sports).

8. Mark Platte, "'Perfect!' timing and a lot of hustle," Honolulu Star-Advertiser, Dec. 9, 2007, 3B.

9. Associated Press Sports Editors, "APSE ethics guidelines," April 21, 2009, apse.dallasnews.com/main/codeofethics.html.

10. Society of Professional Journalists, "Code of Ethics" (Indianapolis, IN: Society of Professional Journalists, 2014).

7

Asking the Questions

The big game is finished. Confetti is flying everywhere. Bands are playing. Fans are screaming. Players are dousing the coach with whatever is in the big water jug on the sideline. Pure celebratory mayhem.

Meanwhile, on a makeshift platform stands one of the winning team's star players. He is wearing a championship hat and hoisting the championship trophy. At least a dozen microphones and tape recorders are dangling in front of his smiling mouth. Television cameras are zooming. The audience is waiting to hear from this happy champion.

Then, it happens. On cue, one of the dozens of reporters will begin the brief post-game interview session with the time-honored question:

"How does it feel?"

You have heard that question before, right? Has a player ever responded by saying, "It feels horrible," or "You know, Samantha, it really doesn't feel as exciting as I thought it would. I was expecting more"?

Of course not. "It feels awesome!" or "I've never felt this!" are the predictable responses.

Is it irresponsible or unethical for sports reporters to ask an athlete how he or she feels after the championship game? Well, no. Are there more insightful questions that might elicit better, more telling, more colorful — and less predictable — answers for the audience?

Absolutely.

Eliciting good quotations is the result of good interviewing, one of the finer skills — and one of the most important ones — for good, thorough sports reporters.

Adam Jardy, beat writer for Ohio State men's basketball for the Columbus Dispatch in Columbus, Ohio, offers this piece of advice for sports reporters preparing to ask questions:

Have an original thought.

"Don't be asking someone to write your story for you," Jardy said. "Have an idea. If you know what you're writing or what your thought is, what your take is, then your questions will inform your writing. They won't *be* your writing.

"I'm trying to give people opportunities to express themselves within the context of whatever information I'm looking for. You can't put words in their mouths, and you can't command they talk to you. You need to have an original thought if you want to get any sort of interesting answer."

Jardy also advises reporters to keep themselves out of the question. After all, the story isn't about the reporter.

"I'm the one asking the questions, but I don't need to involve myself into it," Jardy said. "I don't need to be part of the question. People don't care what my thoughts are. They want to know what LeBron James thinks about this. I try to keep myself out of it as much as I can."

INTERVIEWING SKILLS

Interviews are essential to any sports story. Descriptive game stories need reaction from the coaches and participants. But interviews do more than provide emotion from participants.

Sports reporters must remember to ask solid questions to obtain necessary, accurate information for all types of stories. A story on fundraising for a stadium expansion project will require some basic information questions. How much money has been raised? Who has donated? What timelines are involved?

An investigative piece on possible NCAA recruiting violations will require some tough questions for the athletic director and coach and maybe the recruited athletes. Those interviews will likely provide both reaction and information. Feature stories need several interviews for background information and for feeling.

Preparing for Interviews

Several basic principles apply for preparing for interviews. These include

- When possible, arrange interviews at least 24 hours in advance.
- Inform the interviewee of your general topic.
- Write down at least five questions for personal reference.
- Research, research, research.
- Use a digital recorder, but take notes, too.

The No. 1 rule for sports reporters before conducting interviews? Do your homework.

By being informed, you are saving time for not only yourself, but also your interview subject. If you have only 15 minutes to spend alone with the newly hired junior college baseball coach, do not spend the first 10 minutes asking basic background information that, in most cases, you could have researched before the interview.

Instead of asking, "Where was your previous job?" you could ask, "When you coached at Northeastern, how did you manage the rotation two seasons ago when you lost your star pitcher? What did you learn from that experience?"

Not only are you asking a more insightful question, you are showing the coach you care enough and are responsible enough to have done some background work. You showed interest. Sources do notice this.

Most interviews are arranged in advance — ideally, at least 24 hours. (See chapter 8 on how to contact sources for interviews.) The people being interviewed will often ask about the topic, mostly to give them an opportunity to prepare, although in some cases the subject matter might determine whether that source grants the interview request. A star athlete who has experienced personal struggles might be happy to talk about her quest for a school record but not be willing to share thoughts on a close friend's death or relative's illness. If your story is about athletes dealing with off-court issues while in pursuit of greatness, your interview request might be denied. But better to know a day ahead of time rather than wait until a specially arranged interview that produces nothing.

On the other hand, an athlete willing to talk about private subject matter has an opportunity to prepare while not being taken off-guard, and is therefore able to provide more insightful responses.

By arranging an interview ahead of time, sports reporters also give themselves time to prepare intelligent, insightful questions. Write out at least five specific questions. Take them to the interview for personal reference.

Also take your digital recorder, but use a notepad, too. Batteries in recorders can die easily, or a recorder can be lost or broken not long after an interview. There is no right or wrong way of taking notes. Some reporters use shorthand. Others scribble. Some write down key words. As long as you are able to decipher what you have written, that is all that matters. And you want to be able to generate accurate information.

More experienced sports reporters might say they are able to think of questions in their sleep, especially for general, day-to-day interviews on a beat. True, not all experienced beat writers will have a list of questions on their notepads when doing a postpractice interview with a player. But there will probably be an occasional exclusive, sit-down interview with a hard-to-reach athletic director or maybe a famous athlete visiting the area. Writing specific, prepared questions becomes more important in those situations.

PHOTO 7.1
Using a digital recorder is very important in any interview, but be sure to take notes on your notepad, too.
iStock Essentials/toxawww

Not all interviews will allow for heavy research time. Take postgame interviews, for example. Questions will be more impromptu. Still, it is important to be as well-informed as possible. That means paying attention to the event. When a middle-distance runner has just set a school and state record for the fastest 800-meter time — 1:51.59 — at a high school track meet, a question such as, "Is that a personal best time for you?" is kind of embarrassing, especially when the record has been announced repeatedly over the public address system.

Impromptu questions also occur with breaking news stories. When a beat reporter learns a coach has suddenly resigned, he or she will immediately try contacting the coach for an interview, which won't leave much time for writing out questions. Reporters' instincts, however, should kick in, with the general who-what-where-when-why-how questions.

ASKING THE RIGHT QUESTIONS

Any question that elicits a colorful response, an interesting anecdote or useful information is considered productive. Of course, it's hard telling which exact question will produce those desired results. From a journalistic standpoint, a certain question might be considered bad, corny or poorly worded, but if it somehow results in that perfect

LEARNING THE HARD WAY

Interview access for college athletes will vary depending on the school's policies. Some colleges and universities try to protect their student-athletes from too much media hounding and allow for interviews maybe only once or twice a week. Other schools, particularly those that may want more media attention, will be more open.

David Plati, associate athletic director for sports information at the University of Colorado, takes another factor into account when considering the positive aspects of student-athletes doing interviews — the educational experience: "I know when an athlete does an interview, he's going to have a tougher interview later in life than somebody asking about his football accomplishments," Plati said.

Coaches are experienced enough to know what to say and what not to say to the media. But even though many athletes are given a crash course on how to handle interviews, some 18-year-olds can be a little loose and outspoken in front of reporters.

That's when some media relations staffs coil into damage control mode. Plati, though, views those experiences as important lessons for college students.

"People get burned in interviews all the time. Whose fault is it most of the time? Most of the time, it's the interviewee," Plati said. "He said something he shouldn't have said. Don't pin it on the reporter who got the answer you shouldn't have said and ran with it. That's their job.

"You have to live through that experience of being burned, and you live through that by your mistakes."

Most often, those situations involve calling out an opponent and providing the proverbial bulletin-board material. "That's survivable, I think, in the big picture of things," Plati said.

quotation or a lively sound bite, that question wasn't so bad after all, was it? Truth be told, even the "How do you feel?" question, as cliché and predictable as it seems, just might, once in a while, produce something fun and surprising.

That doesn't mean good sports reporters should expect bad questions to generate great results. Most times, they don't.

As veteran freelance sports journalist Mike Babcock said, "There are no bad interviews, only bad questions."

Here's a guideline for asking good questions:

Ask a Question

Sounds simple enough, right? Then do it. Do not make a statement. Statements by sports reporters will most likely contain opinion. Reporters are not there to tell a coach what went wrong in a game. Also, statements are not questions, and therefore do not require a response.

"Coach, your running game really stalled in the fourth quarter, and your offensive line looked tired."

How is a coach to respond? Sometimes, he might elaborate and bail out a reporter who did not really ask a question. Other times, a curmudgeonly coach might respond with, "That's a statement, ask me a question. Next question!"

OK, so let's rephrase.

"Coach, why did your running game produce only four yards in the fourth quarter?"

The coach still might be a little grumpy, but at least he is forced to answer a question and not give you a blank stare.

Another growing trend among sports journalists — and not necessarily a good one — is the "talk about" question, which, of course, isn't really a question at all. Consider this a passive-aggressive demand of your source to spew words about a certain topic.

Reporter: "Talk about your ability to process information. Is that something you've always been able to do?

Marcus Mariota: "I don't know . . ."

Mariota, former quarterback for the University of Oregon, received six straight "talk abouts" in a single news conference before the national championship game in 2015.[1]

Oh, there are others:

"Talk about your game-winning basket."

"Talk about your decision to go for two points in the third quarter."

"Talk about the electric atmosphere."

Talk about, talk about, talk about.

"In general, you should put some thought into your question and the way you phrase it, not just fall back on the lazy convention of throwing out a bunch of words and trying to get the person to say something in response," said Austin Meek, a sports columnist for the Register-Guard in Eugene, Oregon.

Yes, philosophically, your question should be a question rather than instructing somebody to do something. However, sometimes, in the flow of an interview, Meek said he's asked what he thought was a really good question that elicited a really terrible response, and conversely, he's admittedly asked a very lazy question that received a good response.

"Sometimes, it's less about how you craft your question and more about just kind of the tone of the interaction," Meek said.

For example, the week before the aforementioned national championship football game, the question that begat Ohio State coach Urban Meyer's stunned, "Oregon won by 40!?" exclamation was also the result of a "talk about."[2]

Ask Open-Ended Questions

Ask a yes-no question, and you might get a yes-no answer. That is OK if you are simply after pertinent information. "Did you fracture your leg?" and "Will your starting forward be eligible?" are questions that can be answered with one word but still provide needed, useful information.

The situation is different when you are trying to generate longer responses for a useful quotation.

"Did your offense have a difficult time adjusting to their zone defense in the second half?"

Remember the curmudgeon coach? He is not in very good humor, so he will likely answer the question as briefly as possible: "Yes. Next question."

That didn't get you very far, did it?

A better approach would be to use an open-ended question, or a question that asks an opinion or interpretation from the source. The source is open to respond in any way.

"What difficulties did their zone defense give your offense in the second half?" or "How did their zone defense affect your offense in the second half?"

A closed-ended question limits the source's response. It's like a question with a multiple-choice answer.

"Do you prefer coaches with loose coaching styles or coaches who are strict?"

How is the player going to respond? Probably by saying, "I like a strict coach" or "Give me a coach with a loose approach."

Again, the better approach is to change the question so it's open-ended.

"What coaching style do you prefer?"

This allows the athlete to respond in many ways, and might generate a better response.

Don't Ask Leading Questions

Whereas open-ended questions allow for sources to respond freely with their opinions, leading questions take the opposite approach. Leading questions are questions that try to lead the source to respond in a certain way. Much like statements, leading questions can be dripping with opinion. Sometimes, they are obvious clues a sports reporter has already drawn his or her own conclusion on a subject and is merely trying to gather quotations that will support his or her angle.

"Joe, you're probably happy to see a change in coaching staffs, aren't you?"

This question is leading Joe into responding about what the reporter perceives as positive aspects of a coaching change. That seems to be the reporter's angle, anyway. That doesn't mean Joe necessarily has the same opinion. Sure, Joe is free to dispute the question, but he might go along with the line of questioning and give the response the reporter wants.

Instead, the sports reporter should make the question open-ended.

"Joe, what are your thoughts on the change in coaching staffs?"

Now Joe is able to respond freely.

Ask Follow-Up Questions

Remember the five questions you wrote out in advance? Those do not have to be — and probably should not be — the only questions you ask. They are merely something to get the interview started.

Do not be afraid to stray from the path after even one question. That first question might elicit a response that requires another question or a follow-up question. Follow-up questions might be needed to clarify a response. They might help encourage the source to expand on a thought or anecdote that you find interesting or helpful. They might seek further information.

"You just said your foot has been bothering you. What's wrong with it? When did you hurt it?"

Sometimes a simple follow-up question can change the course of an entire interview, and perhaps the angle of your story. A follow-up question could also lead to a sidebar, separate story or an item in a notebook.

Pay Attention and Observe

Sometimes, sports reporters become so focused on asking the right questions and searching for good answers that they can miss the obvious.

Interviewers should always pay attention to nonverbal signs. A roll of the eyes might indicate disgust. A smile might be a sign of sarcasm. A player answering questions while staring at the ground throughout the postgame interview might be distraught. These are all signs of emotion that sports reporters could describe in order to give life to a story.

Observations should not be limited to the interviewee. Look around. The coach's desk might be cluttered with game film and scouting reports. That might help describe the coach's frenzied week in preparing for the big game. Fans might be gathering outside the locker room, waiting for the player you are interviewing to finish and sign autographs. Fans who've trespassed the field postgame and are handcuffed in makeshift jails underneath the stadium could make for an interesting sidebar or note.

INTERVIEW SETTINGS

The types of questions sports reporters ask might depend on the interview setting. If it is just you and your source, you will probably ask questions in a more conversational setting. A large group of reporters might limit your number of follow-up questions. News conferences usually produce more general questions.

One-on-One Interviewing

It's just you and your source. It is the best possible setup for a sports reporter, but one that requires the most work and research.

You are the only one asking questions, so you better have a good plan. The advantage is the exclusivity: No other reporters are present, so there is always a chance for a breaking news item or scoop, even if the interview was meant for a simple feature.

Small Group and Postgame Interviews

Have you ever seen a television interview in which an athlete is standing in front of his locker with a bunch of tape recorders and microphones in his face? Postgame interviews can truly be a mad scramble, or scrum, and a hectic time for sports reporters on deadline.

For newcomers, some postgame interviews involving a small to medium group of reporters can be intimidating. Squeeze your way into the huddle with your tape recorder or camera. Be assertive but polite. Speak up with your questions. Do not dominate with too many questions, but do not let other reporters ask all the questions either.

In some instances, you might be hopping from player to player, from huddle to huddle, scrum to scrum, trying to gather information from as many sources as possible. The experience can be stressful and, at the same time, exhilarating.

Role Reversal

Sports reporters will often find themselves on the other side of interviews.

Sports talk radio shows love to pick the brains of the local beat reporter the week before the big football game to get any inside information, insight and predictions. Sports reporters might ask each other questions about a hotshot recruit on a weekly vid-cast or podcast on a newspaper's website. Fans might even have an opportunity to ask questions of sports reporters on a live internet chat or through Twitter.

Sometimes it's good practice to be on the receiving end of questions. And it's kind of fun to be the one saying, "No comment."

Other times, a postgame interview might be a quiet one-on-one interview. Or, what begins as a one-on-one interview might suddenly grow into a group. Be prepared for either scenario.

Most colleges and high schools will conduct postgame interviews in a designated room or area and not allow reporters in locker rooms. (The policy differs in professional sports, where most locker rooms are open to reporters, men and women, of course.) Reporters will corner athletes in a hallway by the locker room, outside the team bus or even underneath the stadium bleachers. The setup is not always ideal, especially when the marching band goes by or fans from the opposing team stop to yell obscenities. Be ready to deal with distractions.

PHOTO 7.2

Beat writers take their laptops to home, press boxes, coffee shops — anywhere, really, when the news breaks.

iStock Essentials/poike

News Conferences

The most formal of interviews, news conferences are designed for sources to share information simultaneously with a group of reporters. News conferences are more structured and organized than small group interviews.

The source, not the sports reporter, is in control of a news conference. Most news conferences begin with opening statements from the coach or athlete. Sports reporters will follow with questions. News conferences can last anywhere from five minutes to half an hour or longer, depending on the subject or circumstances. On some occasions, the source will simply appear long enough to make an announcement and not take any questions. The source, or a person representing the source, such as a sports information director, will usually decide when the news conference ends.

Some tips for dealing with news conferences:

- Arrive ahead of time. News conferences might start early, and it's awkward and a little embarrassing if you are scurrying around a room, finding a place for your tape recorder and searching for a place to sit when the coach is already talking. What's worse, you might miss the biggest news.
- Pay attention. Sometimes those weekly media luncheons with the football coach might be a little boring and make you a little sleepy (especially after eating the free pizza), but stay alert. Never ask a question that has already been asked.
- Be cognizant of what you ask. Remember, the answers to your questions are fair game for all members of the media. If you are working on an exclusive story, do not ask questions that might tip other reporters. If possible, save the in-depth questions for a one-on-one interview.
- Be considerate. Do not dominate the news conference by asking a string of questions. Keep the follow-up questions to a minimum. There might be more time to spend with the subject after a news conference, but don't depend on it.

Many times, postgame news conferences are broadcast live via closed-circuit television, with a feed going directly to the press box. This allows sports reporters on a very tight deadline to listen to the coach and players and gather a couple of quick quotations before filing the story. The drawback is those reporters are merely listening to questions and answers and not participating. But when a trip to the interview room and back might take too much time on deadline, listening to and watching a telecast is a good option.

Generating Original Content Through Interviews

Many reporters, especially columnists, will go to great lengths to interview sources one-on-one in an attempt to gather as much original content as possible.

Original content, in other words, is information that consumers didn't hear in the news conference that all of the other reporters, and the audience, just heard.

"The harder you work to get the person one-on-one, the better your work is going to turn out, especially when so much of what we do is in the group setting, whether a press conference or scrum," Meek said.

"I think it comes through. I think readers can tell when you put in the effort to get something that not everybody else has, and something where the person feels like it's more conversational. If you can get somebody away from the group, I think that comes through in the way they talk and when you read the quotes on the page, people can pick up on that."

How do you secure a source off to the side, alone?

It's not always easy, and it's especially difficult the higher-profile the source is. A high school coach may be much more willing to visit alone with a reporter than somebody with the popularity and demand as, say, New England Patriots quarterback Tom Brady.

"Part of it is having the courage to stop somebody and say, 'Hey, can you talk to me for two minutes?' It doesn't have to be a 30-minute, face-to-face, one-on-one," Meek said.

Reporters hoping to grab a source after a news conference or similar group setting are always scouring the territory. Where will the source go after the main interview? Where will he or she walk? Where should the reporter be in a natural position so as not to have to run after the source in some awkward, obvious way?

And don't be offended if the source brushes off your request for exclusivity. It's happened to all reporters at some time or another.

"You develop the ability to just shake it off," Meek said.

As mentioned earlier, reporters should also realize that what they ask in a group setting is fair game for all competing reporters to use. Whatever the source says is available for all reporters, not just the one reporter who asked the question.

To that end, reporters are sometimes leery of whether to ask a question in a group setting. Sometimes, it depends on the nature of the question. Those questions of a more private nature, reporters would never ask in front of a group, and the sources are generally appreciative of that gesture. Use common sense and discretion.

And if you ask a question that elicits breaking news or a profound quotation in a group setting, realize you don't have exclusive rights.

"I think we've all been there, where we've gotten to ask a question that there was some great response, and you're like, 'Ugh, I wish only I had that,'" Meek said. "But we've also been on the other side of it, where somebody else asks something that we used. In some ways, we all borrow from each other and depend on each other."

Sometimes reporters may find it necessary to bypass the chance for a one-on-one interview after a news conference and take their chances on reaching that source through a phone call or text message later that day. Reporters usually have some sort of contact information for sources on their beats (see chapter 8), sometimes with rules or restrictions on when or when not to use it.

Responses will vary, of course. While some sources, particularly coaches, will answer (eventually) every single phone call or text from a reporter, others are less dependable.

In the one season Willie Taggert served as head coach of the University of Oregon football team, Meek estimates he sent Taggert some 20 text messages. The coach didn't respond to a single one.

"The fact he didn't respond didn't keep me from sending a text message the next time," Meek said, "if I thought there was something I needed to talk to him about."

Electronic Interviewing

Although not the preferred means to interview a coach or athlete, sometimes the only option for interviews is via electronic means. Telephone interviews are the most acceptable form of electronic interviews. Sports reporters can ask questions and generate responses but are not able to see nonverbal signs, which is a drawback.

News teleconferences are also common. They operate on the same principles as a news conference, only via telephone. Reporters dial a number, and when prompted, a moderator opens one reporter's line for a question. All reporters who are dialed into the conference can hear the questions and responses. Remember: Keep your speakerphone on mute when you are not asking a question. Nobody wants to hear your barking dog or crying baby in the background; and if an interviewee does hear something, be prepared for him or her to comment.

Interviews via email or Twitter or any form of social media should be used as only a last resort. When a source has time to read through a written list of questions, the answers are wordy and sound scripted. Also, follow-up questions might not be possible, and there are no nonverbal signs. Of bigger concern is the interview's authenticity. It is hard to be 100 percent certain your source is the one who provided the answers to your questions, and not an agent, coach, friend or sports information director. Inform your readers when you have conducted an interview via email or social media.

The internet can also be a helpful tool with interviews. Those postgame news conferences with a live feed to the press box are many times broadcast live on the internet. (They are also often archived.) A beat reporter covering a university's athletic department might cover the hiring of a former athletic director at a new university. When that new school is 2,000 miles away, and the news conference to announce the hiring is scheduled to begin in 90 minutes . . . well, even a company Learjet might not save the day. But watching the news conference via the internet is an option. The reporter will not be able to ask questions but will at least be able to listen, gather quotations and write a story on what happened.

USING QUOTATIONS

Quotations add flavor, detail, emotion and information. Without them, sports stories would be nothing but play-by-play accounts of games. Features would be a long narrative. Breaking sports stories would be a string of facts and numbers.

Fans want reaction and insight. What did the coach think of his decision to go for the two-point conversion in overtime? Why did the wrestler suddenly change his strategy? How did the volleyball players react when learning their victory qualified their team for the state tournament?

Quotations allow sports reporters to tell a story through sources while remaining neutral. You are quoting sources with opinions or general thoughts that you, as a reporter, should not express.

Types of Quotations

Direct Quotations

A direct quotation is an exact, word-for-word account of what a person says. It is enclosed in quotation marks and is attributed to the source. Direct quotations should be used to convey a person's emotion or opinion. The more colorful, the better.

> "The pitcher has got only a ball. I've got a bat. So the percentage of weapons is in my favor and I let the fellow with the ball do the fretting."
>
> — Hank Aaron

> "You can't sit on a lead and run a few plays into the line and just kill the clock. You've got to throw the ball over the goddamn plate and give the other man his chance. That's why baseball is the greatest game of them all."
>
> — Earl Weaver[3]

> "Just take the ball and throw it where you want to. Throw strikes. Home plate don't move."
>
> — Satchel Paige[4]

Of course, not every quotation will be as lively or entertaining. Still, try to use quotations that reveal something interesting. Do not quote clichés. Sports reporters are discouraged from writing clichés, so why quote a coach or player using one?

"We've got to take it one game at a time."

"He really brings a lot to the table."

"This was a total team effort."

Sigh. These quotations add nothing to your story and might bore your reader to sleep.

Quotations that include numbers and statistics are also unnecessary.

"Clay scored 18 points, but 10 of those came in the fourth quarter and gave us a lift. He made all six of his free throws."

If you are covering that game, you should know how many points Clay scored and when he scored them. Having the coach repeat that information to you in a postgame interview does not benefit you or add any spice to your story.

Numbers can appear in quotations, though. Sometimes a source talking about statistics can be colorful and insightful, like this one from Mickey Mantle:

During my 18 years I came to bat almost 10,000 times. I struck out about 1,700 times and walked maybe 1,800 times. You figure a ballplayer will average about 500 at bats a season. That means I played seven years without ever hitting the ball.[5]

Paraphrases

A paraphrase summarizes what a person says without changing meaning. Because it is not word-for-word, a paraphrase does not have quotation marks. Reporters might paraphrase to shorten a long quotation that can be summed up in a few words or to better explain a quotation that may otherwise be confusing.

Take the following direct quotation from Duke basketball coach Mike Krzyzewski.

I think the experience of having been in those situations in the conference, really in over half of our games, we have been losing or just about to lose. It is tough to simulate those types of situations and you have to experience them. So far this year we have experienced them in a positive way and again you're experiencing them today. Our team turned it into something positive, which is good toughness on our part. [6]

The general thought this coach is trying to convey can easily be relayed in a paraphrase.

Krzyzewski said his team has benefited from playing in many close conference games and has become tougher.

There. You have used 17 words to explain what Krzyzewski took 76 words to say. Now you have more room to detail the game-winning basket or squeeze in an interesting note.

ATTRIBUTION

When reporters attribute, they are crediting a source for information. Direct quotations and paraphrases are always attributed. The preferred verb of attribution is "said."

> "If a tie is like kissing your sister, losing is like kissing your grandmother with her teeth out," George Brett said.[7]

Why stick with "said"? It is clear, concise and neutral. It does not imply. It does not offer opinion. It cannot be misinterpreted. It is safe and all-inclusive.

Inserting other attributive verbs in place of "said" can change meaning or imply a source's emotion that might not be accurate.

> "This is the worst game I've ever seen this team play," he snapped.

> "We have got to be more aggressive in the second half," she insisted.

> "Bygones are bygones. The hard part is over," he exclaimed.

"Exclaimed" insinuates he shouted. "Insisted" sounds like she was pretty tense. And did he really "snap"? Your definition of "snapping" might differ greatly from your readers' or your source's definition.

Some sports writers may feel compelled to substitute and switch attributive verbs so the story does not become boring. Don't. It is OK to use "said" repeatedly. Readers do not pay close attention to attributive verbs anyway. They simply want to know who is speaking.

Here are some commonly overused or misused verbs of attribution that writers should avoid:

asserted	remarked	declared
cautioned	explained	opined
quipped	charged	claimed
recalled	maintained	shouted
warned	noted	added
went on to say	continued	pointed out

Style, Placing Attribution

Here are some style rules for using direct quotations:

Use a comma inside quotation marks before the attribution, and use a period at the end of the attribution.

Correct: "Coach always says if you set a good screen, you're more than likely going to be the one getting the wide open shot," Perry said.

Incorrect: "Coach always says if you set a good screen, you're more than likely going to be the one getting the wide open shot." Perry said.

Incorrect: "Coach always says if you set a good screen, you're more than likely going to be the one getting the wide open shot", Perry said.

Use subject-verb order with attribution.

Correct: "That last play was just luck," Smith said.

Incorrect: "That last play was just luck," said Smith.

Use only one form of punctuation at the end of a direct quotation.

Correct: "How many times is this going to keep happening to us?" he said.

Incorrect: "How many times is this going to keep happening to us?," he said.

Use a period after the attribution, and conclude the quotation with a period inside the quotation marks. (For direct quotations that are longer than once sentence, it is best to insert the attribution after the first sentence, then continue with the quotation.)

Correct: "Football is what I've got," Sam Keller said. "Football is what I love and what I'm good at. What you have and you love, you need to embrace. You realize what you love to do, and you get a fresh start at it."

Incorrect: "Football is what I've got," Sam Keller said, "Football is what I love and what I'm good at. What you have and you love, you need to embrace. You realize what you love to do, and you get a fresh start at it."

Incorrect: "Football is what I've got. Football is what I love and what I'm good at. What you have and you love, you need to embrace. You realize what you love to do, and you get a fresh start at it," Sam Keller said.

Use single quotation marks to separate quotations within quotations.

Correct:	"He came to me and said, 'I don't know,' and he said he didn't feel good. So, I said he wasn't going to play."
Incorrect:	"He came to me and said, "I don't know," and he said he didn't feel good. So, I said he wasn't going to play."

Sometimes, direct quotations may be several sentences. Quotations may be divided into paragraphs, but if your quotation lasts longer than two paragraphs, it had better be a good one.

When a quotation covers more than one paragraph, do not use quotation marks at the end of paragraphs, until the quotation is complete.

Correct:	"I thought it was an extremely hard-fought game," Roy Williams said. "Both teams really wanted to play well, but their team played better than we did. They were the most disciplined team on the game tonight.
	"The team that did the most of the little things won the game tonight. Whether it is shooting the ball in the hole or making free throws in the second half or getting a hand up on the outside shot — the team that won the game was the most disciplined.
	"They did the best job doing what their coaching staff wanted them to do."[8]

Quotations should always be paragraphs to themselves.

CLEANING QUOTATIONS

Not every "uhm," "yeah" or "ya know" needs to be included in a direct quotation. Sports reporters are allowed to omit the stumbles, so long as the meaning is not changed.

The Associated Press stylebook says to "never alter quotations, even to correct minor grammatical errors or word usage."

"We was happy to win the game," he said.

That might sound like fingernails on a chalkboard to some, but if that is what the player said, that is what should be written, according to the Associated Press. However, local style may override this rule.

Sometimes, direct quotations may include profane words. In such instances, writers should use the first initial of the profane word, followed by dashes.

"Their season went to the s———.
That one kid, he hasn't done s———.
He's back, but he got his f————
a—— kicked," he said.

Writers might want to shorten a direct quotation rather than use a paraphrase. It is OK to take out repetitive, unnecessary words — as long as the quotation's thought or meaning stays the same — by using an ellipsis to indicate omitted words.

Perhaps a writer wanted to directly quote Krzyzewski, but not all 76 words.

"I think the experience of having been in those situations in the conference. . . . It is tough to simulate those types of situations, and you have to experience them," Krzyzewski said. "So far this year we have experienced them in a positive way, and again you're experiencing them today."[9]

LOST IN TRANSLATION

I once had an assignment to interview a delegation of Chinese youth track officials who were coming to Lincoln to watch a Junior Olympic meet.

I called the university and asked if they had any interpreters. They said, "Sure," and the guy would meet me when I interviewed the Chinese.

He got there early and I thanked him for coming. He said he was happy to help me meet the Japanese team. I corrected him and said I was meeting with Chinese officials.

He said he didn't speak Chinese. The Chinese didn't speak English. He said he'd try.

I asked a question, such as, "How many youth track programs do you have in China?" He would muddle through something. My answer coming back was something along the lines of "Chinese have a great history of track and field."

I'd ask the next question, something along the lines of, "What is the experience of your delegation in running track programs for youth in China?"

The answer was "23,756."

Another question like, "Do you like the weather here?"

The answer, "Our youth programs are growing by leaps and bounds."

— Ken Hambleton, Lincoln Journal Star

Quote Sheets

Transcribing your interview — listening to your digital recorder or iPhone voice memo, and typing out every word your source spoke — can take time, sometimes twice as long as the interview itself.

That is time well spent.

Having your own quote sheet, or a written transcription of direct quotations from a source or sources, is helpful when you are trying to determine which are the best direct quotations, which quotations you would rather paraphrase and which quotes probably will not make your story.

While writers create their own quote sheets for personal use, sports media relations staffs also often release quote sheets after news conferences and events. These quote sheets can be helpful if you don't have time to transcribe a 45-minute news conference, are trying to search for that perfect quote on deadline or perhaps weren't able to attend the event. Usually, the questions (or question topics) and answers will both be on these quote sheets.

Quote sheets from other outlets are helpful and permissible but should be used with some caution. The person transcribing the interview might not be as thorough as you when it comes to a word-for-word account. Words may have been inadvertently omitted or changed, and not all quote sheets are a complete account of what was said. Also, media relations staffs who make quote sheets are likely to leave out controversial or confrontational material that may have occurred during the news conference.

Be aware of spelling, and realize that quote sheets may not adhere to AP style and may contain run-on sentences.

UPON FURTHER REVIEW

1. The university athletic director has called a news conference to begin in two hours. You only know the topic is "a change in direction for the baseball program." What steps should you take to prepare for this news conference?

2. Your editor returns your feature story on the freshman All-American gymnast and says it's filled with too many quotations. How do you determine which quotations to keep and which to omit? What are other options?

3. Los Angeles Dodgers pitcher Clayton Kershaw is in your town for a fundraising event and is gracious enough to do a 10-minute, one-on-one interview with you later the same day. How do you prepare? What types of questions will you ask? Why?

NOTES

1. Bryan Curtis, "The Worst Question in Sports: What We Talk About When We Say 'Talk about,'" Grantland, Jan. 22, 2016.

2. Curtis, "The Worst Question in Sports."

3. Quotes from website quotemountain.com, www.quotemountain.com/quotes/sports_quotes/baseball_quotes/.

4. Quote from website https://ftw.usatoday.com/2014/11/15-best-sports-quotes-of-all-time.

5. Quote from website quotemountain.com, www.quotemountain.com/quotes/sportsquotes/baseball_quotes.

6. Quote from postgame news conference, Feb. 6, 2008, Duke University sports information.

7. Quote found on the website brainyquote.com, www.brainyquote.com/quotes/quotes/g/q131189.html.

8. Quote from postgame news conference, Feb. 6, 2008, Duke University sports information.

9. Quote from postgame news conference, Feb. 6, 2008, Duke University sports information.

Working With Sources

You've probably heard of a youth basketball coach who conducts the season's first practice — or maybe two or three practices — without even tossing a basketball onto the court.

The idea is to show the players how the game of basketball involves more than dribbling and shooting. It's about running, hustling, setting screens, playing hard-nosed defense, doing the grunt work.

Fans may not notice or appreciate those things on game day. Still, that extra work is vital to the overall success of the team. Without it, the final product — the game — will not be top quality, and fans will wonder what is wrong.

The same concept applies for sports reporters. There is more to the job than writing stories, much like there is more to basketball than shooting and dribbling. Audiences expect a high-quality product but don't really care about or understand the legwork involved.

Sports reporters have ample legwork to do before even opening a laptop or picking up a camera — developing and working with sources, staying informed, keeping abreast of developing situations, creating story ideas and working with schools' and teams' media relations departments.

That's why media outlets create beat writers.

BEAT REPORTING

A beat reporter is a reporter who covers the same team, sport or league on a regular basis. Beat reporters are common at newspapers and electronic media websites, which divide sports and teams into individual beats.

Having the same reporter responsible for covering one team makes sense from an organizational standpoint. Less confusion exists within the sports department over who is covering what. Also, having a beat reporter makes it simpler and faster for the team or school when contacting an outlet's sports department with general information or breaking news. Readers are better able to relate to coverage when the same person is providing stories.

Some beat reporters follow the same team for years. Other times, outlets will shift duties and reassign beats, mainly to keep reporters from getting too comfortable and to give readers a fresher, different viewpoint from another beat reporter. There is no steadfast rule on this; it simply varies from outlet to outlet.

Sometimes a beat reporter covers more than one team or one sport. A high school beat reporter may cover dozens of area high schools. A college beat reporter might follow only one school but be responsible for covering several sports with that school. A beat reporter for the Big Ten Conference will cover multiple schools and multiple sports.

Beat reporters are sometimes responsible for a variety of sports beats. The same person covering the local Division I-A football team might also be responsible for local horse racing coverage in the summertime. A women's college basketball beat reporter could double as the men's gymnastics beat reporter, even though the seasons overlap. It can be a delicate balancing act.

Conversely, a beat might be too large for one person to handle. Some newspapers will put two or three reporters on the same beat. That's when communication becomes critical among beat writers and editors.

Responsibilities of a Beat Reporter

A beat reporter has access to a team that fans do not. Part of the reporter's responsibility is to take fans where they cannot go by providing as many details and as much information as possible. Who is injured? Which players are surprising coaches with strong practice play? Which assistant coaches are on the road recruiting? Is the head coach considering another job?

Beat reporting isn't simply writing features and traveling to games on the company's dime. Those are just the highlights. Thorough beat reporters have the daily pulse of the team they cover. If somebody asks you where the head coach is making a public appearance Thursday night, or for which postseason awards the star quarterback is a candidate, you should have a knowledgeable answer.

A primary goal of a beat reporter is to be the first to provide accurate news to the audience. Beating competing media outlets to a breaking news story is known as getting a scoop. Another goal for beat reporters, then, is to not get scooped. And if all competing outlets break the story within the same reasonable time frame? Well, a tie isn't a win, but it is certainly better than a loss.

A beat reporter's busiest time is in-season. Football beat reporters are busy from August through November. Basketball beat reporters live in gymnasiums from November to March. High school beat writers follow whichever sport is in season (or sometimes three sports) for a school year and then begin the cycle again come fall.

But the off-season is when some beats, especially those involving college teams, have the most legwork. Coaching changes, roster moves. Recruiting, recruiting and more recruiting. Some beats, because of avid fan bases, are year-round. North Carolina basketball and Alabama football fans crave news about their programs every day of the year. With limited access and resources in the off-season, finding stories and keeping tabs on the goings-on within a team can become more challenging for a beat reporter.

That is when developing and maintaining sources becomes especially important.

Cultivating a broad range of sources can take weeks or months for a new beat reporter. The process is never-ending. Beat reporters are constantly updating their email contact list and adding numbers to their cellphones. It is virtually impossible for beat reporters to thoroughly cover the same team on a regular basis without the help of sources.

PRIMARY SOURCES

Primary sources are most important. These are people who have information or opinions that are vital to the outcome of your story. Coaches, players, athletic directors or management are all considered primary sources for any beat reporter. Game stories will almost always contain information gleaned from interviews with coaches and players.

Charles Richardson had hoped to emerge from a pile of humanity in time to shake the hands of his opponents.

He was too late. By the time Richardson's Nebraska teammates had finished dog-piling their team captain and hero, stunned Texas Tech players had quickly trotted off the court.

"I ain't ever been in that situation before," said Richardson, whose three-pointer at the buzzer lifted Nebraska to a dramatic 61-59 victory over Texas Tech on Tuesday night at United Spirit Arena.

Should Richardson find himself in a similar situation, he hopes he and his teammates can hold their composure a little better.

"We needed to show more class," Richardson said of Nebraska's dizzying celebration on the south end of the court. "I know how it feels to lose like that. I know we were all excited, but I was trying to get the guys up off me."[1]

Richardson, the player who made the game-winning shot, is the obvious primary source.

A story about a player being suspended from the team will have essential information from the coach — why the player is being punished, how long the player will be suspended and what the terms of the suspension are. Coaches make those decisions; therefore, they are the primary sources in such circumstances.

When players break records, reach milestones or are honored with prestigious awards, they become primary sources. Fans want to know their thoughts and reaction, no matter how predictable the response may be. Can you imagine a story on the Heisman Trophy winner without any words from the winner himself?

The best-written stories include multiple primary sources. A story about a coach's future employment with a team, or possible loss of employment, needs information from more than the coach. In fact, the coach, while still considered a primary source in the situation, may be reluctant to divulge details.

Reporters need to contact athletic directors or management to ask questions about possible contract negotiations. A "no comment" response is possible but sometimes just as telling.

The coach's agent also becomes another primary source. Agents many times serve as spokespersons in lieu of the coach and might provide clearer details. In feature, investigative or other sports news stories not necessarily related to a beat, primary sources will vary, depending on the topic.

Local businesspersons and investors become primary sources for a story about a city trying to attract an independent baseball team. An off-the-wall feature story on sports internet message-board junkies cannot be told without talking to the junkies themselves.

In these cases, the primary sources are not necessarily people whom reporters work with on a regular basis or with whom they have a strong relationship. But they are essential to that particular story.

SECONDARY SOURCES

Think of secondary sources as condiments to a hamburger. You could probably survive without them, but they certainly add much-needed flavor and zing. Secondary sources are just that: secondary. They are not essential to the outcome of a story but add information that makes a story more complete.

That story about the Heisman Trophy winner? Members of his family might be able to share an entertaining anecdote or two to spice up your story. His teammates could probably attest to his work ethic or competitiveness. Reaction from fans on the street can give your audience another viewpoint.

Secondary sources are most common, and perhaps most important, for longer, in-depth feature stories. They also ensure your audience that you are not being lazy and producing one-source stories — stories that are told using only one primary source. Unless it is a breaking news story or deadline story, you should tell your story using more than one source. After writing the first version of that story, try to update with more sources and rewrite. Stories on websites can be and are constantly updated.

A short feature story on the 12-year-old baseball player with one arm could easily be told after you talk to just the player himself. But why stop there? Secondary sources — his teammates, opposing players, parents, spectators — will give your story much more depth . . . and save you a scowl from your editor.

Material Sources

Not all sources are people. Material sources are physical items such as record books, media guides or perhaps even other stories that can provide information for a reporter.

A sports reporter filing a report after a game must have the leading scorers and preferably other statistical information that would appear on a postgame box score or statistical sheet. A writer working on a biographical story on the new assistant volleyball coach will likely turn to the school's media guide.

A feature story on the five women's volleyball players living together in the same house will probably have several quotations from the players themselves. Perhaps the reporter wants to include some historical perspective and research other instances of teammates housing together. A material source might be the archives — a website search or perhaps a look into the libraries of local newspapers. Yes, they still exist!

Be careful, though. Just because material is archived does not mean it is 100 percent correct. Archived material — past stories, clips — should be verified for accuracy.

Behind-the-Scenes Sources

Not all sources will appear as a prevalent part of your story. In fact, some sources may not appear in your story at all.

Behind-the-scenes sources are people who provide pertinent information or ideas for stories but are not necessarily used as primary, or even secondary, sources in your actual story. For beat reporters, developing behind-the-scenes sources is a key part of keeping up with the goings-on within a program.

How many times do you hear a student manager, team trainer or player's roommate quoted in a story? Probably not often. But those people can still be useful to sports reporters. In many instances, they are more involved with the team than you are and probably have access to some information you do not.

Behind-the-scenes sources go beyond managers and trainers. Boosters and friends of the program, former players, athletic department personnel — anyone who is around the team with access you might not have — can help. Behind-the-scenes sources need to be knowledgeable, trustworthy and dependable. They could provide you with some key information that leads to a breaking story. However, information you glean from behind-the-scenes sources needs to be verified with a primary source before you can write a story.

On the Record Versus Off the Record

Sources who talk to reporters are doing so with the assumption they are speaking on the record — meaning everything they say in the presence of a reporter is fair game for a reporter to use in a story and attribute to that source.

If a reporter wants to speak off the record — meaning the conversation and information gleaned from it cannot be used or attributed in a story — the source must clearly state he or she is speaking off the record. Sometimes, entire conversations can be off the record, if clearly stated at the outset.

Reasons for speaking off the record are numerous and, most times, understandable. In the case of behind-the-scenes sources, they are usually trying to protect their own status or employment. Primary sources, such as head coaches, may want to give you some background on why a player is struggling but may not want the information public. This is where trust between sources and writers is paramount. What happens if a reporter burns a source and uses off-record information in a story? Chances are, that source won't ever trust you again, and you've lost an essential part of your beat building.

What good is off-the-record information if you cannot use it? That is where good sports journalists implement their reporting skills.

Let's say you are a beat writer for a college football team. Daily practices are closed to the media, but you are invited to conduct interviews after practice. With 100-plus players dispersing at once, it is possible you did not notice the first-string running back was absent.

That is when a good relationship with a team manager becomes helpful. He might alert you, off-record, that Joe Smith was injured in practice. Now privy to the information, you ask the coach, who must address the situation on the record. Information gathered on the record can be used in a story, and the source can and will be identified.

The coach becomes the primary source in a story or notebook item about Smith needing an MRI on his injured knee. But information from a behind-the-scenes source, the manager, helped produce the story, even though he is not mentioned. This is also known as a news tip.

ANONYMOUS SOURCES

In the case of the injured running back, it's pretty simple. You are tipped about the injury, off the record, from your behind-the-scenes source. You gather information, on the record, from your primary source, the coach, and produce your story.

MOMMA KNOWS BEST

In the wild season of 1994, Nebraska's football team lost quarterback Tommie Frazier early on to blood clots. Not long after, his backup Brook Berringer suffered a collapsed lung during the first half against Wyoming.

He recovered enough to finish the game but was taken to the hospital. I followed up with a visit to the hospital after I filed my game stories.

Walking into the emergency room, I saw Frazier, there for blood testing. I asked what he saw. "I saw Brook come through here on a stretcher. I don't know what's going on."

Nobody was giving out information. I stepped outside to think about what to do. I asked a woman what she was doing there. She said her son was in the hospital for a collapsed lung. Mrs. Jan Berringer shared her fears and her hopes with me for the next hour.

— Ken Hambleton, Lincoln Journal Star

Easy, right?

Not all situations are so tidy. Usually, the bigger or more scandalous the story, the harder it is to prod your primary sources to talk on the record when broached with the subject.

What then?

That is when any of your sources can become even more essential under the cloak of anonymity. Anonymous sources are unnamed sources that become your primary sources, mostly in breaking sports stories. While not ideal, stories with anonymous sources — sometimes just referred to as "sources" — have become more and more commonplace in today's sports media world.

Some newspapers, however, still use extreme caution with anonymous sources. Some still require that more than one anonymous source be used in such stories, and those sources must be independent of each other.

The decision on whether to run a story with unnamed sources is not taken lightly. Writers and editors meet and discuss variables of the situation.

- What is the news value?
- Who are the sources?
- Can they be verified?

- How dependable are they?
- Is there absolutely nobody who will speak on record?

The risk of running stories with unnamed sources is understandable. What if the sources are wrong? Even the most trustworthy and knowledgeable people are capable of mistakes. Remember, a reporter's credibility is at stake and could be forever damaged.

Then again, what if you have a major scoop? Breaking a story about steroids use or an impending big coaching change might boost a young reporter's career and give a news organization some notoriety.

Even when stories with anonymous sources turn out to be correct, they still might not be popular in the public's eye.

The Lincoln Journal Star once cited three anonymous sources and reported Nebraska's head football coach, Frank Solich, would be asked to retire at season's end. The story was splashed across the front news page of the Sunday newspaper, a week before Nebraska's final regular season game at Colorado.

> Athletic Director Steve Pederson wants Frank Solich out as Nebraska's head football coach, according to three sources close to the situation.
>
> Pederson will try to persuade the sixth-year head coach to formally announce his retirement following NU's Nov. 28 game at Colorado, offering him a job in the Athletic Department and a lucrative buyout package, said the sources, who agreed to talk on the condition they not be identified.
>
> "He wants Frank gone. He's made up his mind," said a longtime, out-of-state booster with close ties to the department.
>
> The sources said Nebraska's first-year athletic director reached his decision eight days ago, after watching fans stream for the exits early in the fourth quarter of Nebraska's 38-9 loss to Kansas State, its worst home defeat in 45 years. The blowout, NU's second on national television this month, appeared to bore ABC sportscasters before the network cut to a more competitive game. It also came on the heels of Pederson's Nov. 6 news conference announcing a $40 million fundraiser for new athletic facilities.

> "Texas and Kansas State weren't competitive games. They were the straws that broke the camel's back," said a Texas booster also with strong ties to the program. After the K-State game, the source said, Pederson walked to the skyboxes to reassure boosters that "we're going to do something, don't get upset."
>
> Pederson denies he's spoken to anyone about a plan to force Solich's retirement, and some of the program's biggest boosters deny they've ever heard that plan. Former Coach Tom Osborne said he hasn't spoken to Pederson about such a plan.
>
> "I am on the record as saying I have not discussed this matter publicly or privately," Pederson said at the Devaney Center Saturday night, where he was attending the NU men's basketball season opener. The athletic director declined to comment further. Solich also declined to comment.[2]

The backlash included the Journal Star building being egged. Hate emails. Critical letters to the editor.

Among the complaints and concerns were that unnamed sources should not be quoted, for they may have hidden agendas. The newspaper was irresponsible in its reporting and showing a lack of respect for Solich. The newspaper was engaging in sensationalism and simply trying to sell more papers. Using anonymous sources is unethical.

But the story turned out to be true. One week later, the large headline across the Sunday front page read: "Solich fired."

> Nebraska football coach Frank Solich was fired by Husker athletic director Steve Pederson Saturday night in a meeting at South Stadium.
>
> Pederson called Solich into the athletic director's office at 7:30 p.m. and told him of the decision, according to Solich's daughter, Cindy Dalton.
>
> "Pederson told Dad that he really hadn't made up his mind until five minutes before Dad walked through the door," Dalton said. "Dad said he

> couldn't believe that Pederson had the nerve to say that to his face."
>
> Solich, 59, was fired one day after leading Nebraska to a 31-22 win over rival Colorado in Boulder. That gave the No. 25-ranked Huskers a regular-season record of 9-3 overall and 5-3 in the league.
>
> Last Sunday, the Journal Star, citing three anonymous sources, reported Pederson would try to persuade Solich to announce his retirement after the Colorado game.[3]

Sometimes, a potential source will contact a beat reporter with information that could lead to a breaking sports story or perhaps a scoop. That is another example of a news tip. Reporters should make every effort to confirm and identify the source, who might anonymously call or email. Regardless of whether reporters can identify the source, they must verify the information through one of their regular primary sources, secondary sources or, in some cases, behind-the-scenes sources — anyone who can verify whether the newfound information is true.

When the University of Michigan conducted a football coaching search, coaching candidates began surfacing. One such candidate, the Lawrence (Kan.) Journal-World reported on its website, was then Kansas coach Mark Mangino. The newspaper reported that Mangino's agent had released a statement saying Mangino was in "serious negotiations" with West Virginia.[4]

The source was not anonymous. But it also was not real. A man claiming to be Mangino's agent had released a similar statement to several media outlets and also made phone calls to reporters, trying to convince them of this "news." The elaborate hoax tricked the Journal-World, which did not verify whether the man was actually Mangino's agent or check the origin of the released statement.

The newspaper ran a correction and apologized for misleading readers — an embarrassing, yet lesson-providing mistake that could have been prevented by making a couple of phone calls to verify the source, rather than rushing for a possible scoop.[5]

Contacting Sources

So you have begun to cultivate some sources — primary, secondary and behind-the-scenes.

- How do you reach them?
- When do you talk to them?
- How often?

Much of that will likely depend on the reporter's beat and the available access. A high school beat reporter overseeing an extensive coverage area might have dozens of coaches to contact on a weekly, biweekly or maybe monthly basis, depending on the number of schools and sports involved (and the number of reporters). It likely requires a couple of phone calls to the school — maybe to a secretary, maybe directly to the coach, maybe to an assistant. High schools, depending on their size and location, will vary on their policies (if any exist) for interviewing coaches. Coaches, in turn, might set ground rules for interviewing athletes.

A phone call to the coach's home or athlete's home might be more common on the high school level — again, depending on the school's size. The coach of a Dallas metro high school football team might keep an unlisted phone number. A reporter might find — and interview — the coach of a small-town West Virginia girls' basketball team at the downtown bowling alley.

Contacting collegiate and professional coaches and athletes can be a little more involved. Beat reporters generally have a set standard time for interviewing coaches and players — before practice, after practice and after games, or during a specially arranged time.

Colleges and universities set guidelines, usually listed in their media guides, for non-beat reporters or visiting reporters to arrange interviews. The drill usually goes something like this:

> Contact the sports media relations department at least 24 hours in advance with the interview topic and request. Most reasonable requests, but not all, are granted.

PHOTO 8.1

Sports news conferences are for all types of media, where every microphone is fair game to use any quote, no matter which reporter asks the question.

iStock Essentials/razihusen

Be aware: Coaches are known to suddenly, and without reason, cut off media access to players. It might be for a day. It might be for a week. It's usually not a regular occurrence, but when it happens, beat reporters must quickly adjust.

Being a beat reporter can be a rewarding experience. In some rare instances, though, it can be a nightmare. Sometimes, individual athletes will make themselves off-limits from media. Some want to focus, some do not want the attention and some just plain do not want to deal with reporters. The higher the level of sport, the more likely that is to happen.

RELATIONSHIPS WITH SOURCES

Relationships With Coaches

Beat writers should develop solid, working relationships with sources, particularly primary sources like coaches. You will be working with them on a regular basis, so establishing and maintaining a strong relationship is important.

How does that happen?

When you are new on a beat, make an appointment to introduce yourself. Tell the coach a little about yourself — your origin, where you have worked. Discuss the working relationship you hope to establish. This does not need to be a long meeting, just long enough for the coach to know who you are and what you will be doing.

Chances are, the coach will lay some ground rules — when you may contact him, how you may contact him and what his policies are for interviewing athletes. Some coaches might give you a personal cellphone number with instructions on when and when not to call it. Others might give a stern lecture if you ever (1) find out his cellphone number or (2) have the audacity to call it.

The ideal relationship is one in which the coach and beat reporter have as many off-record conversations as they have on-record interviews. That's not very common. Many coaches, especially on the college and professional levels, are hesitant to share off-record information with reporters for fear they will see it appear on-record anyway or maybe find it on social media outlets. (See chapter 7.)

Other coaches may be more forthcoming and trustworthy. If a coach eventually does feel comfortable enough visiting off-record with you, then, by all means, do not burn him or her by leaking the information or, worse yet, reporting it.

Not every meeting with a coach needs to be an interview. Sometimes it's good to visit, off-record, about other subjects, other sports and other teams. It can be an icebreaker at the beginning of a working relationship and will allow you to see each other's nonworking side. Such conversations can help build a general rapport.

That does not, however, mean beat reporters should be "buddy-buddy" with coaches or other primary sources. In fact, getting too friendly is not a good idea. It could create an obvious conflict of interest.

What happens when a high school football coach — the same guy you've begun hanging out with at the local pub — gets into trouble with the law? Would you approach that story any differently than you would if the same thing happened to that other high school football coach across town . . . the one who has been sort of gruff to you in past interviews? Of course, it is easy to say you would be the consummate professional and be 100 percent impartial. Explain that to the fan who has seen you and the coach hanging out at the pub after games.

Perception is everything.

Public encounters with sources can and do happen. Just understand the fine line between what is appropriate and what is not, and the potential ramifications if you cross the line.

There will be — and should be — times when beat reporters and coaches will not agree. How a beat reporter deals with these instances depends on the situation and the coach. Most times, a short meeting clears the problem. With more severe issues, it might be necessary for third parties — sports editors, athletic directors — to become involved.

Whatever the problem, it is important to communicate and come to some sort of resolution. Having a beat reporter and a coach constantly at odds is not good for either party.

Relationships With Athletes

Relationships with athletes will differ depending on the level of sport you are covering. You are not likely to have as much day-to-day contact with high school athletes as you might with athletes on a college or professional team. Part of that is because high school beat reporters are usually responsible for coverage of several high schools, making it more difficult to have regular personal contact with so many athletes.

Age also is a factor. High school athletes may not be as mature when it comes to interviews and dealing with reporters. Therefore, you are not as likely to develop a working relationship. The extent of your contact may be postgame or postmeet interviews.

Exceptions may be if you are covering a very high-profile high school athlete or if your beat is college recruiting. Then your primary sources are 16-, 17- and 18-year-olds, and developing some sort of relationship, no matter the athlete's maturity level, is important.

For a college beat reporter, developing relationships with athletes becomes more important. Any one of them, at any time, may become a primary, secondary or behind-the-scenes source, and sometimes all three.

If you are new to the beat, introduce yourself to as many athletes as possible. Usually, reporters have access to athletes either before practices or after practices, depending on the team's or school's policies. If a team has open practice, attend as often as possible and as long as possible. When you are visible to athletes, they will not only have an opportunity to get acquainted with you but will also see and appreciate your interest and willingness to know what's going on. Yes, they will notice.

Be friendly and conversational in interviews. Strike up conversations or make idle small talk with players — the ones you normally interview, and even the ones you don't. Walk-ons enjoy some attention, too. Over time, players will know and, ideally, trust you. Those relationships might be helpful when you need some inside information.

Athletes are like coaches — some will relate with reporters better than others. That is expected. As with coaches, there will be times of friction with athletes. Especially on the collegiate and professional level, not everything you write will be glowing and positive. Nor should it be. Some athletes who are upset with a particular story, or the media in general, might begin declining interviews or brush off your attempts at small talk.

While it is usually not good to have an athlete avoid you, it's not as critical as having a coach cut you off. In most cases with disgruntled athletes, your best and probably only choice is to let them be. Most times, they will come around. If not, you have others to turn to for that sound bite or quotation.

And, as with coaches, never burn an athlete as a source, and don't get too friendly with the star point guard.

WORKING WITH MEDIA RELATIONS

As journalists, reporters are obligated to produce fair, unbiased stories for their audiences. Media relations personnel, meanwhile, are obligated to their employers to present them in as positive a way possible in any information released to the media. Each needs the other, yet each regards the other with a healthy attitude of skepticism. Both work diligently to build trust and strengthen working relationships that make it possible to meet each other's needs.

Reporters depend on sports information directors and media relations personnel for access to much of the information they need to produce game and season stories, and sports information directors and media relations departments depend on reporters to report positive news about their teams, players and programs into the media.

Sports information directors and their staffs serve as liaisons between a school's athletic department and the media and public. General duties include assisting media with coverage by providing statistics, notes and information on a school's teams, arranging interviews with athletes and coaches and organizing game-day operations.

Some colleges and universities prefer the title of sports media relations director. The job description is the same, although the specific responsibilities of sports information directors, also known as SIDs, may vary. "You might get 20 different answers if you asked 20 different SIDs," said David Plati, associate athletic director of sports information at the University of Colorado.

Sports information staffs at larger schools, like Colorado, generally include seven or eight full-time staff members, one or two graduate assistants and a host of undergraduate students. Each person is assigned one or two sports, sometimes more.

Plati's office is responsible for media guides, weekly and daily news releases, game and meet programs, statistics, record maintenance, game and match administration, general correspondence, and speaking engagements. But, as Plati writes in his 19-page office manual for student assistants, every office has its own way of running its show.

Colorado's sports information office issues, on average, more than 400 news releases or information updates per year. When Plati began his current position in 1984 — he was the nation's youngest sports information director — that meant coming in on Sundays, typing four to eight pages of football notes, copying, folding and stuffing them in envelopes, and rushing them to the post office.

"And everybody was seemingly happy when they got it in the mail on Wednesday. Now, if somebody called on Sunday and said, 'Hey, I need your stats,' and we said, 'You'll get them on Wednesday in the mail,' that would not fly," Plati said.

Writing for Sports Information

Plati, who teaches a course in sports public relations, says weaning students from a grandiose style of writing is usually his first challenge.

"It's like they're writing for highlights on ESPN," Plati said. "They're trying to build this crescendo to get to the score. State your case in the first paragraph, what it is, and throw in what I call the grabber, that one fact that spices it up. Whether it's the guy on the internet reading it on our website, or if you're sending your story to a sports editor, do you want to read seven paragraphs in before you find out what the hell this is about?"

Don't overwrite, either, Plati advises in his office manual. A release full of mundane and useless information is filed in the wastebasket or deleted from email.

Sports information writers generally take a positive approach, even when that task may seem difficult. "You lose a football game 70-3, there's no way to put lipstick on that pig," Plati said.

Pointing out the negatives, in those cases, is sometimes necessary and should be done carefully and tactfully. "You've got to be smart, but don't be critical of your own team," Plati said.

If your team goes 6-of-20 from the free-throw line and loses by three points, it's hard to ignore the fact that poor free-throw shooting was to blame. Sports information staffs emphasize to their writers that they should, if possible, try to get a coach or player to say something about the free-throw shooting so it can be used as a quotation.

"If none of them say it, you can point it out by saying, 'The major difference in the game was CU missed 14 free throws and had their worst night of the year at the free-throw line.' That's perfectly acceptable," Plati said.

Highlighting or dwelling on the negatives, however, isn't acceptable. Plati said he remembers taking his class to see the NBA's Denver Nuggets play. The students' assignment was to produce three pages of game notes. Some students put two negative notes on the first page. "In my class you'd get a D or an F. You know what you get from [Nuggets owner Ann Walton] Kroenke? The pink slip. You don't make fun of your own product."

Media Guides

One of the biggest projects for any sports information department is writing and designing media guides for each sport. Media guides, a popular material source for sports writers, also serve as recruiting guides for prospective student athletes, so information is vast.

For media members, media guides contain records, biographies, game and season summaries, schedule information and general media information, such as how to arrange interviews, apply for game-day credentials or find a motel in the area.

Media guides vary in length depending on the sport. For many years, college football media guides boasted the honor of being the largest. Before the National Collegiate Athletic Association began mandating that all media guides be no longer than 208 pages, some guides had grown to four times that size, with most of the information designed to lure recruits. If nothing else, those guides made good doorstops.

Today, some athletic departments have ceased printing physical guides altogether and share their guides in PDF format on flash drives.

Here's a breakdown of some key information Plati recommends be included in a media guide, with suggestions on how to approach writing certain areas.

Credential Requests

One responsibility of sports information directors is granting credential requests for media members and assigning seats or locations for coverage of games.

Each school sets guidelines on what media outlets are eligible to apply for credentials. For example, beat writers from daily newspapers will receive credentials, whereas freelance writers for fledging monthly magazines might need to cross their fingers and hope for free access.

One unique stipulation at the University of Colorado: Any website that sponsors anonymous message boards is not eligible for credentials. (An exception is made if a printed publication accompanies the website.)

It's part of Plati's fight against anonymous internet posters. "If you want to criticize us, if you want to rip us, that's fine. But you know what? When newspaper people do that, their names are on it. On sports talk shows, when somebody calls in

MEDIA GUIDE INFORMATION

Biographies

- Use basic questionnaires for athletes, coaches and staff.
- Research bios of the person and any other information that can be accessed.
- Research and maintain a record of accomplishments since that form was submitted.
- Provide accompanying photographs (mugshot, action picture).

Last Season/Season in Review

- Game summaries (do as they are played; don't wait until the year is over).
- Statistical summary.
- Key pictures.

Opponent Section

- Schedules/results/pertinent information for each opponent.
- All-time series results (and trends).
- Bests against and by the opponent.

Record Book

- "The Last Time"; perhaps the pages to answer the most common questions.
- Career leaders.
- Year-by-year leaders.
- Select circles/longest plays.
- Single-season/game bests.
- Individual and team records.
- Opponent records/bests.
- Home venue information and records.
- Attendance records.

- Records by season.
- Coaching records.
- Year-by-year results.
- Program milestones/chronology.
- Honors/awards.
- All-American and all-conference nominations.
- All-time letter winners.
- Players in the pros/draft picks.
- Postseason history.
- Bowl, playoff games/tournament results.
- Postseason records.
- All kinds of miscellany.
  - vs. the nation
  - vs. ranked teams
  - television appearances
  - season/conference openers
  - all-time comebacks

Media Information

General information (credentials, parking, access, services, interview policies, etc.).

Website information (links, procedures, passwords, etc.).

Media outlets (major organizations that cover the program on a regular basis).

Media hospitality (listings of hotels, restaurants, rental cars, taxis, etc.).

with an asinine rumor or accusation, you cut the caller off in a second. You never stop criticism. But we want sites to be responsible."

If those sites want credentials to Colorado athletic events, Plati makes them identify their posters to him, if a situation warrants. That includes rivals.com and scout.com sites that focus on Colorado athletics. "And if they don't identify them, the agreement is that if I call them and say, 'Who's Stokes27?' they have to tell me to keep their credentials."

Over a 15-year span, Plati estimates he's only needed to ask about six times for an outlet to reveal the name of a message board poster.

SPORTS NEWS RELEASES

A sports news release, another example of a material source, is the primary communication tool used by organizations, colleges, businesses and nonprofit groups to send information to the media. Sports news releases represent the interest of the sponsoring organization and contain a message the source thinks is news or might be an idea for a news story.

Email is the delivery method of preference for news releases, with fax and mail distant second and third options.

Contrary to popular belief and to the implication in its name that it is news, a sports news release does not communicate news to the public. The goal of a news release is to attract the interest of the media — one editor, news director or reporter at a time.

Media want stories with local angles that will interest their audiences. If a sports news release presents the possibility of such a story, journalists will consider it. If the news release does not make a local connection in the headline or the lead, or contains more fluff than fact, the media are less likely to pursue it.

Why Send a News Release?

Information conveyed through news releases serves three general functions:

- It announces events and personnel changes. A professional sports team or a university athletic department might issue a sports news release when a coach is hired or fired, a player signs or is drafted, a conference affiliation changes or a building project is planned.
- It promotes citizenship and good causes. Athletes partnering with youth service programs, reading to elementary school students or sponsoring a middle school soccer camp are events that promote them as good citizens in their communities.
- It builds a person's or organization's image. Scholarships, awards, promotions and hall of fame recognitions promote a positive image for recipients and sponsors.

SADDLE UP

Ted Harbin spent 20 years in the newspaper business, primarily in sports. Originally from western Kansas, he's also long had a passion for rodeo.

Harbin decided to combine his sports writing, layout and editing experience with his love for a nontraditional sport by beginning his own business: Rodeo Media Relations.

Among Harbin's goals is to not only promote rodeo and its athletes, but to help sports writers better understand a sport some may have a difficult time grasping. Harbin knows it's not an easy sport to cover.

"Most sports writers understand baseball. They understand basketball. They understand football. A few understand soccer, most can wade their way through other sports, like golf and wrestling, but they can't grasp the difference between bareback riding and a saddle-bronc ride."

To that end, Harbin writes what he calls nontraditional news releases. They are more feature-oriented.

"Most of the newspapers I'm sending these things to are going to be your small daily newspaper, where I'm trying to entice editors to say, 'Hey, this is a pretty good story, it's about a local guy.'"

The idea is to inspire local news outlets to follow up with interviews and produce their own stories, although some newspapers, including the Dallas Morning News and Fort Worth Star-Telegram, have used some of Harbin's content verbatim, he said.

Harbin has served as a rodeo correspondent for six newspapers in the Midwest, including the Kansas City Star, and writes for Texas Monthly magazine, both in print and through blogs that appear online. He's either written stories or had news releases appear in hundreds of publications.

Rodeo Media Relations is a multifaceted business. In addition to helping rodeos market their product — much the same way a sports information director does for a football team — Harbin also serves as a publicist for cowboys and other rodeo personnel.

— Brian Rosenthal

Sometimes it's necessary to release news that's not positive. A player is arrested, a coach has been fired, members of a team are killed in a van crash or a franchise is moving to another city. A sports news release makes the official announcement in straightforward, factual language as quickly as possible following the action.

Senders should never use sports news releases to mask an issue or to cover up facts, but they can and do approach the topic from a perspective that makes them look as good as possible.

Reporters who receive sports news releases know the information is generated and distributed by biased sources not obligated to represent both sides of the story.

A sports news release is not a news story and is not meant to be used as such. Reporters check the information carefully and verify the quotations in the release. A sports story or gamer based on information in a news release is rewritten and expanded to present an objective, balanced and fair message. It is converted to AP style as needed.

The media view a sports news release that does not have a newsworthy point, or is filled with puffery in place of fact, as an attempt to get free advertising. If a fresh, newsworthy topic is not the reason for sending a release, don't send it.

Factual information is the most helpful. If the topic has news value, present it in a straightforward news style. Chances are better that a release will be considered if it presents facts and is written in journalistic style than if it is laced with puffery and overblown superlatives a la P.T. Barnum's "Greatest Show on Earth." Not everything can be the newest, the best, the fastest, the most coveted or the only one of its kind.

Journalists also read news releases looking for future stories or photos. The announcement of a women's rowing team being started at a local university may generate a news story. The reporter may also file the release as a reminder to check back for a story on the changes the university is making to accommodate practices and schedule competitions. The dates of the first practice and first meet are noted on the photographer's assignment sheet.

UPON FURTHER REVIEW

1. You've joined your school's newspaper staff and have been assigned to the women's basketball beat. It's August. What immediate steps would you take to prepare yourself for this beat? What else would be on your list of things to do before the season begins?

2. A trusted source informs you of possible NAIA or NCAA infractions on the men's soccer team. When you approach the coach with questions, he wants to know why you're asking and who told you the information. What do you do? How could you prepare yourself for this situation?

3. Interview or job shadow a sports information director for a college or professional team. Prepare a list of questions you don't want to forget to ask. Write a feature news story about the SID.

4. Look at media guides. (You may obtain them from universities or the local sports reporters to whom they are sent.) What content surprised you? What content would you, as a reporter, want to have that was not included?

5. Go to the websites of several colleges, universities or professional teams and look for news releases. Or ask a local television or newspaper sports reporter to save 10 sports news releases for you. Compare the subject lines, format, length and content. What are the similarities? Differences? Which of the 10 would you find most useful if you were a reporter? Why?

6. On the same websites or the websites of local media, find their policies and deadlines for formatting and submitting news releases to them. Compile a list of the contact person's name, email address and fax and phone numbers for media to which you would likely be sending information.

NOTES

1. Brian Rosenthal, "Huskers beat Red Raiders at buzzer," Lincoln Journal Star, Feb. 7, 2007, 1D.

2. Matthew Hansen, "Solich could be forced out," Lincoln Journal Star, Nov. 23, 2003, 1A.

3. Steven M. Sipple, "Solich fired," Lincoln Journal Star, Nov. 30, 2003, 1A.

4. Ryan Wood, "Mangino in negotiations with West Virginia," LJWorld.com, Dec. 19, 2007.

5. Ryan Wood, "Mangino to West Virginia rumors a hoax," LJWorld.com, Dec. 19, 2007, www2.ljworld.com/news/2007/dec/19/mangino_negotiations_West Virginia/ (updated version).

Making the Numbers Count

> "Baseball statistics give many of us our first sense of mastery, our first (and for some of us our last) sense of what it feels like to really understand something, and to know more about something than our parents."
>
> — George Will[1]

Look at the beginning of a not-so-unusual sports story:

> BLOOMINGTON, Ind. (AP) — There was a tense second in the final minute of Iowa's 1-point victory over No. 1 Indiana.

In a game full of thrilling emotions, this writer devoted the bulk of the lead to numbers: one second, the final minute, one point and No. 1 ranking. That sort of preoccupation is not unusual among sports writers. In fact, many of them, and fans for that matter, seem determined to quantify every aspect of their favorite game.

Baseball is perhaps the most notorious example of this obsession. You could probably find, for example, the statistical likelihood of a batter getting a hit in a Tuesday night game at home against a southpaw in July with the bases loaded. Who needs to watch?

From the shelves of bookstores and on the airwaves, telecasts and websites, the number crunchers are out in force. We may be in the golden age of sports statistics. Two companies, the Elias Sports Bureau and Sports Team Analysis and Tracking Systems (STATS), compile data for fans, professional teams and print, broadcast and on-line media around the world. They can tell you worthwhile trivia, such as the fact that a pitcher can reduce the chances of a stolen base by throwing over to first — as well as ridiculously esoteric noninformation, such as which player hit the most foul balls.

PHOTO 9.1
Volleyball statisticians must keep track of digs, blocks and kills.
iStock Signature/FatCamera

What do all these numbers add up to? In sum, they do three things for the intrepid sports writer: They provide new and interesting ways to understand and interpret the game, they provide lots of filler and fodder for radio and TV broadcasters and they help us make smarter bets. Whoops, scratch that last one. Instead, let's say sports statistics help whether we're fans wanting to improve our chances in a fantasy league or players seeking to make a better arbitration case.

UNDERSTANDING THE GAME

If historians were sports writers, we would probably know:

- How long it took Washington to cross the Delaware, depending on whether the wind was blowing up or down the river.
- What size rock David used to beat Goliath, not to mention the brand of his slingshot.
- Why Gen. Custer, given his career record against the Lakota Sioux, should have thought better of participating in the Battle of the Little Big Horn in 1876.

It may seem odd to spend this passion for minutiae on a game, but here we are in a new era of statistical curiosity. There is a statistic for virtually every situation, and a number of astute observers have figured out how to apply all of this numerical data to gain a better understanding of their sport.

Keeping Track

First, though, let's consider how those numbers get compiled in the first place. Most of the time, sports writers try to keep "the book," that is, they keep their own statistics. At a basketball game, for example, they might keep track of shooting percentages, rebounds and free throws.

One of the best things about keeping your own stats is that the process forces you to pay close attention. You learn to be intent on every play and at every moment. Who can know, after all, when the game's turning point will come or what play will signal a shift that turns the game around?

It's true that the home team provides an official scorekeeper, but in the case of high school games, that scorekeeper might be the coach's wife, a teacher, the town dentist or the bus driver. These people are probably reputable, but they may only keep track of made baskets and total points. The scorekeeper might leave, too, before you have finished talking with the players and coaches. If the sports writer wants to look under the hood, so to speak, to see the hidden story of the game — the steals, assists and so on — she or he will need to keep track individually.

In college games, the situation changes. The home sports information staff will likely provide a bevy of scorekeepers, each one responsible for a different statistic. One person, for instance, might record the time each point is made. These statisticians often work in pairs, one reporting the result out loud while the other records it. That way, the scorekeeper never needs to take his or her eyes off the game and risk missing something.

Competing Philosophies

Believe it or not, statistics actually play a role in two competing philosophies of sports coverage. On the one hand, we have the sports writer who is intent on finding the story in the numbers. This writer would typically keep close track of several key statistics, and then, as you might suspect, base the story mainly on those numbers.

Many fans appreciate this kind of writing, but there's a risk that you, as the writer, may rely too much on numbers. You may use a stat, for example, when you don't really need one, when a telling quote or sparkling description might work better.

For example, notice all the numbers in the following description of a girls' basketball game:

> For as cold as Southeast was in the first half, then again in the fourth quarter, it was as hot in the third period. Houser

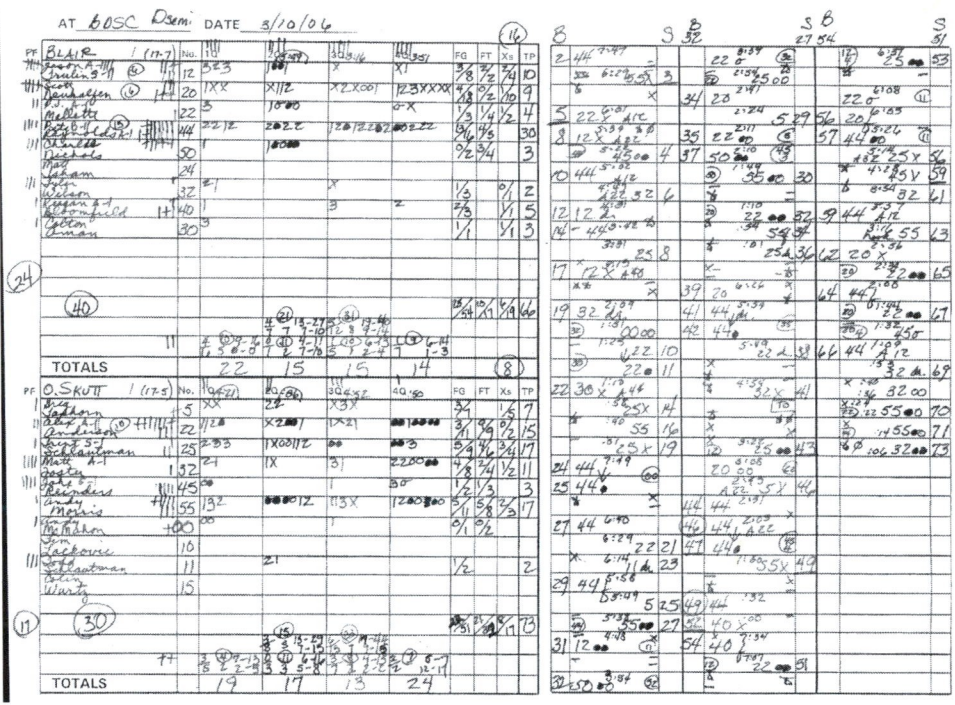

PHOTO 9.2
This page from a basketball scorebook shows how Omaha Central defeated Kearney, 68-58.
Ryly Jane Hambleton, Lincoln Journal Star

hit three 3-pointers, Kastanek tallied 6
points, Katie Birkel chipped in 4, and
the Knights made good on 11 of 15
shots from the field while rolling up
26 points and streaking to a 41-26 lead
after three periods.

That many numbers might make the reader's head spin. Why not just a quote from
the coach:

I don't know how you can play good in
one quarter and not good in three and
still win.[2]

A sports writer with a different philosophy, however, might spurn press row altogether and sit in the stands with a box of popcorn, hoping to catch the flavor of the game
in a different way. This is the writer who notices what the kid on the end of the bench
is doing or gauges the emotions of the fans on each sideline. For this writer, the story is
more about people than numbers.

MAKING THE NUMBERS COUNT   167

WHERE'S THE BIGGEST CLASSROOM?

Students may not get a letter grade for the hours they spend in the weight room and on the running track, but they often swear by the lessons they've learned through sports. The key is finding a good mix between papers and practices, between exams and games. Done well, an intercollegiate athletic program can enhance the lives of all students at the college, whether they suit up for a game or not. "What's the biggest classroom at Carleton?" asks college president Robert Oden Jr.

> People often guess Olin 149, the concert hall, or Skinner Chapel. Almost nobody gets the answer I'm after: Laird Stadium. My point is that lots of teaching and learning happens in athletics.

Varsity athletics tend to teach lessons that are difficult to learn in the classroom. Says former athletic director Leon Lunder,

> Some of the most important things you'll do in life will be done under pressure and in public. You'll have to make decisions without debating or taking time to vote. These are important skills, and you can learn them by participating in sports.

Michael Armacost, former president of the Brookings Institution, a Washington, D.C., think tank, notes,

> I learned the importance of subordinating individual aims to what was good for the team. I learned to hang in there when things got tough, to win with modesty and lose with grace, that luck often played a large role in the outcome of games, and that you can increase the odds of getting lucky by preparing more thoroughly and thoughtfully than your opponent.[4]

Take, for example, this sentence from the renowned writer Murray Kempton, describing a young Cassius Clay (later to become Muhammad Ali) about to enter the boxing ring against the champ, Sonny Liston:

> They met in the ring center with Clay looking over the head of that brooding presence; then Clay went back and put in his mouthpiece clumsily like an amateur and shadowboxed like a man before a mirror and turned around, still catatonic, and the bell rang and Cassius Clay went forward to meet the toughest man alive.[3]

Neither approach is sufficient by itself. The best method is to blend some of each, discovering the key thread of the story through the players themselves and then supporting that concept with facts based on the game statistics.

But don't worry if you feel a bit challenged by the numbers game. As we've indicated, other people are keeping track too, and generally, they will provide the media with frequent updates. At halftime of a basketball game, for example, you will get an update on who's scored, how much, and who's in foul trouble. And after the final buzzer, you've got a box score to examine.

Box Scores

A box score is a detailed summary of a game, usually in the form of a table listing the players and their individual performances. An abbreviated version called a line score basically duplicates the scoreboard on the field.

Baseball box scores may look, on the surface, like nothing more than a list of names and a jumble of figures. But if you know how to read them, you can gather some genuine insights into how a game was played. Many fans check the box scores daily to see how their favorite players are doing or why their team stumbled in the ninth inning to lose a close game.

Study the box score printed below and then answer the following questions:

1. What was the final score of the game?
2. In which inning did the winning team score the most runs?
3. Who were the winning and losing pitchers?
4. How many runners did Mudville leave on base?
5. Which batter had the most hits? Who did the most to raise his batting average?
6. Who were the pinch hitters?

7. How long did it take to play the game?
8. How many fans attended?
9. Who was the only batter to hit a triple?
10. Whose performance is most significant to use in writing a lead?

MUDVILLE	ab	r	h	bi	SPRINGFIELD	ab	r	h	bi
Orson, rf	4	0	1	0	Colbert, 1f	3	1	1	0
Lesco, ph	1	0	0	0	McHale, cf	4	0	2	2
Wylie, cf	4	1	0	0	Kerr, 2b	3	1	2	0
Madden, 3b	4	2	1	1	Carr, 1b	4	2	1	0
Thomas, 1b	3	1	2	0	Van Dyke, rf	3	1	0	0
Kane, 1f	3	0	1	1	Lathrop, rf	1	0	0	0
Panza, c	4	0	0	1	Peterson, 3b	4	0	1	2
Gomez, 2b	4	1	1	2	Polson, c	4	0	2	2
Davis, ss	4	0	2	1	Jones, ss	3	1	3	0
Roberts, p	1	0	0	0	Andre, p	2	0	0	0
Minello, p	1	0	1	0	Knight, p	1	0	0	0
Clayton, p	0	0	0	0	Quinn, p	0	0	0	0
Gray, ph	1	0	0	0	**Totals**	32	6	12	6
Totals	34	5	9	6					

Mudville	000	200	120 — 5
Springfield	011	003	10X — 6

E — Davis, Kerr. DP — Mudville 1, Springfield 2. LOB — Mudville 5, Springfield 6. 2B — Carr, Polson, Jones. 3B — Colbert. HR — Gomez (1). SB — Jones (14). HBP — by Andre (Roberts). T — 2:53. A — 30,649.

Mudville	IP	H	R	ER	BB	SO
Roberts (L)	5.3	8	5	3	3	3
Minello	1.6	3	1	1	2	1
Clayton	1	1	0	0	0	0
Springfield	IP	H	R	ER	BB	SO
Andre (W)	6	5	2	2	1	5
Knight	2	5	3	2	2	0
Quinn	1	0	0	0	0	2

INTERPRETING THE GAME

Everything about the United States seems to be getting larger, from the portions in fast-food restaurants to the size of a chocolate chip cookie. And it's no different in the National Football League. Consider this: The average weight for pro players in 2006 was 248 pounds, 10 percent higher than in 1983. More remarkably, in 1976 just three NFL players tipped the scales at 300 pounds; by 2006, 570 players, or one in five, weighed that much.[5]

IT'S ALL JAPANESE TO ME

During one football season, Kansas State opted to have its home football game against Nebraska moved to Tokyo for the Tokyo Bowl — for a $1 million guarantee for both teams.

While staying in Tokyo for six days, I got a feel for the city. I was assigned to do a Christmas shopping story in downtown Tokyo for the news side. I explained that Japan was not a Christian country to my editor, but to no avail.

But back to the game.

It turned out that my stats would be the official stats for the game since nobody involved in the game, from the Japanese side, understood that stats were important. Thank goodness, I had a long history of keeping my own stats at high school games.

The other "hardship" was the fact that there were five flights of stairs and no elevator between the press box and the locker rooms.

Deadlines being what they were — the game was over at 3 a.m. home town time — it meant writing a running lead and sending. Then, down five flights of stairs for quotes from coaches. Back up the stairs, a side bar and quotes inserted into the lead. Back down the stairs for another side bar on a couple of players. But they had left.

I ran outside the stadium, into this open market, and spotted them. After a loud whistle, they came, provided the quotes I needed for a side bar.

All was peaceful.

— Ken Hambleton, Lincoln Journal Star

Do these numbers tell us anything beyond the fact that almost everything is getting bigger? They may, if we know how to interpret them, and interpreting numbers has been a lifetime obsession for Bill James.

James is a baseball statistician who has written more than two dozen books devoted to an objective analysis of how baseball could and should be played. The Boston Red Sox raised a few eyebrows when they hired James in 2002, hoping to somehow end a streak of 86 years without winning a World Series. Guess what? Since James has come on board, the Red Sox have won baseball's championship twice.

PHOTO 9.3
Track and field races are often measured in the hundredths of seconds.
iStock Signature/FatCamera

Sometimes called the "professor of baseball" or the "sultan of stats," James began trying to work out baseball puzzles at his job as a night watchman in a pork-and-beans plant in Kansas. It was a good job, in the sense that it gave him a lot of time to keep to himself and think about baseball. Each day, he lugged his "Baseball Encyclopedia" and a stack of box scores to his boiler-room post and compiled evidence that began to challenge baseball's sacred cows. He concluded, for example, that starting pitchers have no effect on attendance, and that ballplayers peak in their late twenties.

By hiring James to be their senior baseball operations adviser, the Red Sox joined the ranks of several teams — such as the Oakland A's and the Toronto Blue Jays — that are now emphasizing mathematical data as an alternative to relying on weather-beaten scouts with radar guns and seat-of-the-pants hunches. James calls the effort "the search for objective knowledge about baseball."

In his first "Baseball Abstract," James wrote that he wanted to approach the subject of baseball "with the same kind of intellectual rigor and discipline that is routinely applied, by scientists great and poor, to trying to unravel the mysteries of the universe, of society, of the human mind, or of the price of burlap in Des Moines."[6]

He treated his readers to an egghead's theory of winning baseball, in which outs should be avoided at all costs and walks are really as good as hits. The result of this analysis indicates, James says, that sacrifice bunts are almost never worth the price, confounding a century of baseball's received wisdom.

Do the Math

Remember that algebra you did in high school? Dust off those old formulas because sometimes you will have to plug some numbers into your calculator. Give these a try:

1. Julie Martinez, star shortstop for the Spitwads, has been at bat 77 times this season and gotten 24 hits. What's her batting average?
2. In 37 games, knuckleball pitcher Slim Dickens has thrown 186 innings and given up 47 earned runs. What is his earned-run average? (Hint: ERA is the number of earned runs given up per nine-inning game.)
3. Javon Wilson, North High's star tailback, has gained 812 yards rushing in the first six games of an 11-game season. If he continues at the same pace, in what game will he break the school record of 1,406 yards gained in a season?

Numbers to Note

In putting together a package for an upcoming girls' state basketball tournament, writers compiled a column of "numbers to note." Some of those numbers include teams' winning percentages, number of sophomore starters, returning state champions, unbeatens, first-time qualifiers, top scoring average per player, average margin of victory and longest winning streak. The column was helpful both to sports fans and other sports writers.

FEEDING THE FANS

So who needs to know this stuff, anyway?

Basically, television and radio broadcasters need it to fill the dead air between pitches, plays and serves. According to statistician Gary Gillette, more than 500 stats were discussed by network announcers or displayed on the screen during just one World Series game.[7]

Reading a stat sheet has become an occupational requirement. Besides a dictionary and a thesaurus, many sports writers now study an endless stream of numbers, charts, diagrams and box scores. Those box scores, by the way, have doubled in size as statisticians have added more and more items to measure.

So while most sports fans probably don't know how to fix the plumbing or where their septic tanks are, they can prove that a certain player's first pitch will be a strike more than 60 percent of the time. Some know their favorite baseball player's batting average to one one-thousandth of a point.

DOLLARS AND CENTS

Although "Show me the money!" was just a catchphrase from a Tom Cruise film, it's now a common refrain among sports writers. You may find yourself writing about contracts, buyouts, lease arrangements and the cost of field turf, to mention just a few.

Take this interesting example: College towns have become desirable places to live. People love the pageantry, tradition and idyllic settings of these towns and like to connect with the nostalgia they feel for their own happy college years. So if you decide to write a feature about this topic, you might wonder which college town has the most expensive houses and which has the cheapest.

The answers, according to Coldwell Banker, are Stanford and Ball State. A modest four-bedroom home with a double garage in Palo Alto, California, home of the Stanford Cardinal, will set you back about $1.7 million. Meanwhile, a similar house in Muncie, Indiana, home of the Ball State Cardinals, would only cost $150,000.[8]

ARBITRATION SUITS

Certainly sports writers and fans love their stats, but, it turns out, lots of players do, too. Awash in numbers, mesmerized by details such as pitch counts and runners in scoring position, some players have found their value escalating, depending on how the numbers play out. "We'll sometimes get involved in arbitration. Players want stats that will make them look good while teams provide some stuff that will make 'em look not so good," said Don Zminda.[9]

Players haven't always been the masters of their sums. Columnist George Will recalls the more innocent days of the past: "Honus Wagner, the greatest shortstop ever, rejected a salary offer from the Pirates of $2,000 by declaring: 'I won't play for a penny less than fifteen hundred dollars.'"

ITSY-BITSY

Can sports writers get carried away with minutiae? It seems so. Reporters covering a college football team's opening game thought they had asked just about every possible question until someone asked the team captain if he would be calling heads or tails at the pregame coin flip.

The captain took the question in stride and said he had been practicing since "I messed it up in church softball this summer." For the record, the captain said, "Tails never fails."

An NFL running back got those numbers confused not long ago when he said his goal was to gain 1,500 yards or 2,000 yards, "whichever comes first."[10]

FOR THE RECORD

Compiling a sports record book at your school can be a tremendous resource for future reporters. Such a book includes team and individual records for each sport your school participates in over time. For example, suppose you wanted to know the fastest time anyone at your school had ever swum 50 meters or the highest anyone had ever vaulted or the farthest someone had thrown a discus. The record book should be able to provide the answers.

It's often fascinating to look back in history and discover that your tiny college once played Notre Dame in football (or perhaps the local high school). Remember, too, that records are made to be broken. Your sports record book will need to be updated each season as new marks are established.

UPON FURTHER REVIEW

1. How large a role should statistics play in how a reporter covers a story?
2. How can statistics be used to interpret or better understand a game?
3. List ten different statistics you could compile for a sports event at your college.
4. Discuss which statistics seem most significant when analyzing a specific sport.

ANSWERS TO DO THE MATH

1. .312
2. 2.27
3. the last game (11th)

NOTES

1. This quote appears in "The Pythagoras of Winchester, Kansas," a chapter in George Will's book "Bunts" (New York: Scribner, 1998), 54.

2. This game was reported in the Lincoln Journal Star.

3. This quote is reprinted in "The Best American Sports Writing of the Century" (Boston: Houghton Mifflin, 1999), 700. More on the Clay-Liston fight can be found in Kempton's article "The Champ and the Chump," New Republic, 1964, also reprinted in "The Best American Sports Writing of the Century."

4. Erin Peterson, "Fair Games?" Carleton College Voice, Summer 2006.

5. More information about how everything is getting bigger in the United States, including the size of NFL players, can be found in "Livin' Large," compiled by Jess Blumberg, Katy June-Friesen and David Zax in Smithsonian, September 2007.

6. This quote appears in Ben McGrath, "The Professor of Baseball" (New Yorker, July 14, 2003). The first "Bill James Baseball Abstract" appeared in 1977.

7. Gary Gillette is co-editor of both "ESPN Baseball Encyclopedia" and "ESPN Pro Football Encyclopedia." He has written or edited more than 50 baseball books.

8. Coldwell Banker ranks the affordability of housing in major college football towns annually. The study can be found at http://hpci.coldwellbanker.com.

9. Zminda works for STATS (www.stats.com), one of the world's leading sports information companies.

10. Will, "Bunts," 57.

10

Seeking Justice

Sports has long been an important battlefield for human rights. Seven years before the U.S. Supreme Court banned segregation in the public schools, major league baseball brought Jackie Robinson onto the playing field. That decision paved the way for countless other players of various ethnic backgrounds to get their chance to play, and that struggle for justice continues: In April 2018, officials in Boston renamed a street next to Fenway Park. Instead of "Yawkey Way," named for Tom Yawkey who was the last owner in baseball to sign a black player (in 1959), the street will revert to its original name, Jersey Street.[1] The world of sport, it seems, has often been in the vanguard of social change, whether it be the right to play, or as we will see, the right to play safely. To cover this additional dimension, reporters need a few more tools in their kit.

Those tools include at least a working understanding of tax law, criminal law and a variety of other legal and business disciplines that may have been on the periphery in years past. As one observer put it with an eye to future litigation, "When they add rules, even rock throwing becomes a sport." In this chapter we will explore a few of the rules that shape the contest — especially those that determine who will play, and when and under what circumstances. In particular we will focus on three key issues: Should players be paid to play, should men and women have equal sporting opportunities and are some sports simply too violent?

IS AMATEURISM OUT OF DATE?

Modern college sports programs have evolved from 19th-century, student-run social and athletic clubs into powerful enterprises that generate billions of dollars in revenue each year. The scale of the revenue is what is new. The first intercollegiate athletic contest was actually a boat race — a rowing competition between Harvard and Yale on Aug. 3, 1852. The sponsor of the event offered both teams "lavish prizes" and "unlimited alcohol," an attractive reward, we can imagine, to undergraduates. Preparations and training were perhaps less rigorous than today; the Yale team spent the

PHOTO 10.1
Harvard beat Yale by a "few" lengths in the first college sports competition.
iStock Essentials/36clicks

day fishing and "abstaining from pastry," while Harvard avoided practicing for fear of "blistering their hands."[2] Despite a broken oar, Harvard won by two lengths, or maybe four lengths, no one quite knows for sure. Remarkably, this annual race has been held 151 times since.

By the way, the first college football game was played on Nov. 6, 1869, between Rutgers and Princeton.[3]

NCAA Supervision

The activities of college sports programs are supervised and coordinated by the National Collegiate Athletic Association, an organization that regulates the activities of some 400,000 athletes and staunchly protects both the principle of amateurism and the NCAA's own sometimes dictatorial prerogatives. One persistent point of contention is the very concept of a "student-athlete." The term was invented by the NCAA's former director, Walt Byers, in 1953, who thought athletes should be "patriots"; they should play the game for the love of glory rather than out of greed as paid "mercenaries." But Byers' golden rule does not easily describe the rough-and-tumble life of today's college athletes who may not have entered an ivy-covered campus for the sake of a traditional education. Perhaps too often, educational institutions have found it easier to seek national distinction through competition on the field than in traditional academic pursuits.[4]

One of the biggest bugaboos in the NCAA's recent past has to do with endorsement deals. Players have been quick to notice that commercial interests were selling T-shirts and every other kind of souvenir with their name, number or picture — and not a penny was going into their pockets. The NCAA, however, has long resisted any "play for pay" plan. Still, the organization may be looking for a little wiggle room in its long-standing position on amateurism. NCAA President Mark Emmert said, "There's a lot of discussion about the Olympic model, and [I] think it's well deserving of serious consideration inside the context of college sports."[5] Players could perhaps earn money through endorsement deals that are part of the existing contracts colleges already have with clothing and shoe companies. Additional money could come from deals with local and regional businesses. Much of the details of such plans, however, will probably have to be worked out in the court system.

Off to the Slopes

One of the rare instances where an athlete took the NCAA to court involved Jeremy Bloom, a world-class skier who also happened to be a member of the University of Colorado football team. Bloom was making about $1 million a year through sponsorships and endorsement deals, money he said he needed to fund his international travel for skiing competition. But the NCAA determined that any endorsement money would result in the "commercial exploitation" of a student-athlete[6] and that Bloom couldn't take the money and still play football (a rule that changed in 2015). Since that time, athletes have been battling over what financial benefits should be available to them.

Many people consider the idea of amateurism to be an outmoded Victorian concept that belongs to another time and place — such as the early 1920s as depicted in the movie "Chariots of Fire," where a few athletes from the University of Cambridge trained and competed in the Olympics (partly by running around the college courtyard). Today, public institutions use the concept to hold down personnel costs by limiting the money that could be paid to players while still collecting the staggering profits made by their games. Many athletes will eventually leave college without their degree. What if their benefits were dictated by the market instead, and not limited to what the NCAA determined would keep the players "amateurs"?

Youth Basketball Troubles

The issue is not simply about athletes in college. Consider the Elite Youth Basketball League, a Nike-sponsored summer program for high school players. The players travel long distances to play other elite teams several weekends during the summer months, with their expenses and most of their clothing paid for by shoe companies. The activity prompted the NCAA to appoint a commission to discover whether any under-the-table payments were being made illegally to the young players, who were already being aggressively recruited by college programs.

The commission found that many of the high school travel teams had received tens of thousands of dollars in shoes, uniforms and travel money.[7] College coaches were not allowed to attend the games, but they could watch games being streamed on their laptops. "If you're a company and you can sell that, sell this league, sell the format of it, kids are going to buy it," explained Brad Beal of the Washington Wizards.[8] The conclusions that the commission reached were not encouraging. "The corruption we observed in college basketball has its roots in youth basketball," former Secretary of State Condoleezza Rice, who headed the commission, said. The commission called for more transparency from summer camps, but the reality is that little has changed.

Jenkins Goes to Court

Just imagine what a top college basketball player could make if his compensation was not limited by NCAA rules to tuition, room and board, books and a few incidentals. What if, instead, his value was determined by how many people wanted to watch him play on television? Or see him in person courtside? What if he were paid to attend alumni reunions with fundraising at stake? What if he were to make an appearance at a recruitment event for high school students?

At the moment, these questions are moot, but within the next few years they could become quite real to all the parties involved, thanks to Martin Jenkins v. NCAA, a U.S. District Court case in which Martin Jenkins, a defensive back at Clemson from 2010 to 2014, is arguing that his college compensation was unfairly capped. If the judge finds in his favor, college sports as we know it will undergo a fundamental change. What Jenkins has going for him is a previous decision, the O'Bannon class action suit, where the court found that some NCAA amateurism rules violated federal antitrust laws. Thanks to the O'Bannon case, the NCAA now allows colleges to offer a scholarship athlete the "full cost of attendance" which includes an annual stipend of several thousand dollars. Jenkins' attorneys make the argument that colleges already spend a tremendous amount of money on "what is around the athlete."[9] That includes coaching salaries, expensive stadiums and lavish training facilities. They are able to do so, in part, because they don't need to pay players.

The Jenkins lawsuit seeks to overturn NCAA rules that place a "ceiling on the compensation that may be paid for [college] athletes for their services." If the plaintiffs prevail, colleges may find themselves bidding for athletes' services.

DO MEN AND WOMEN HAVE A LEVEL PLAYING FIELD?

Student athletic programs have also been one of the battlegrounds for the gender wars of the past 40 years. As recently as 1972, only 30,000 college women participated in athletics. Today, that number has increased roughly fivefold, to 150,000. This change reverses a perception of women from spectators in sports to active participants. As Kathryn Clarenbach, the first chairperson of the National Organization of Women, put it, before Title IX, women were expected to "stand decoratively on the sidelines of history and cheer on the men who make the decisions."[10] But after Title IX, they could take their place alongside men on the athletic fields. Consider one example: In 1884 Maud Watson won the first ever Ladies' Singles Title at Wimbledon. Her outfit consisted of a white corset and petticoat, and for her prize she received a silver flower basket. In 2018 Garbiñe Muguruza defeated Venus Williams to win a check for $3 million and then got to wear a purple and gold, circular badge signifying that she is a member of the All England Club, an honorary status accorded to tournament champions.[11]

Splitting the Athletic Budgets

The NCAA understood from the outset that the money for women's athletic programs would come from the men's budgets. But to what degree would women's sports be able to achieve equity with men's sports? The definitive tests for compliance ultimately were established by a court case involving a group of gymnasts at Brown University. In 1991 Brown made some budget cuts, including one that eliminated the women's gymnastics team. The following year, some of those women filed a lawsuit against the university, contending that Brown had failed to meet its responsibilities under Title IX. The charge stunned a Brown administrator and future athletic director, Mike Goldberger: "We always felt that we had done a great job in terms of providing opportunities for women," he said, "because at the time we offered more varsity opportunities than any other college in the country for women."[12]

Goldberger wasn't far off in terms of the total number of men's and women's teams offered at the university, but at Brown female students outnumbered men by about 52 to 48 percent, and their athletic opportunities were not equivalent, or so said the First District Court of Appeals. Eventually, Brown agreed to a settlement that required the university to "strive to make the number of opportunities for women in the athletic enterprise equal to their ratio in the student population."[13]

That standard has remained the rule of law ever since. Institutions are in full compliance with the law if they have substantially the same proportion of female athletes on varsity teams as the proportion of female students in the undergraduate population.[14] The court gave colleges two other options, neither of which has been particularly popular. Part two of the three-part test would exempt institutions from sanctions

PHOTO 10.2
A group of gymnasts from Brown helped put some teeth in Title IX.
iStock Essentials/Petr_Joura

if they could demonstrate a "history and continuing practice" of expanding programs for women. Few schools, however, are able or willing to take advantage of this approach. Finally, an institution could meet its statutory obligations by showing that the interests and abilities of women students were "fully and effectively" accommodated.[15]

At the time, however, the Brown case caused plenty of hostility on campus. Digit Murphy, who was head coach of the women's ice hockey team, said she remembers the tension. "It was hell going through a Title IX battle in the '90s," she said. In her testimony she told the court that "girls hit hockey pucks, girls are great mathematicians, girls check and girls love technology. If you create environments that send such messages to girls, they will come."[16]

Arlene Gorton, a former associate athletic director at Brown, is convinced women's sports are better off because of the case. Gorton recalls that on long-ago Saturdays when the football team lost, alumni would grumble that it had been a lousy weekend. They wouldn't have noticed that all the women's teams playing that weekend had won. She is still not sure how much of that has changed or why some college administrators have failed to embrace simple fairness. "The money could have gone into the programs," she said, "and it confounds me why it didn't go into the programs to bring equity, rather than fighting the case.

PLAY LIKE A GIRL

"Float like a butterfly, sting like a bee," was once Muhammad Ali's mantra for his fighting style, but it might just as well apply to a new boxing club for girls in Pakistan. The First Women Boxing Coaching Camp in Karachi got its start when a 16-year-old girl asked local boxing champion Nadir Kachi to teach her. As more girls became interested, the club began to grow.

"Boys have two arms and legs and so do girls," said Kachi. "So why wouldn't these girls fight just like boys?"

— Katie Booth, "11 stories of female athletes who made their own rules," womenintheworld.com, Dec. 30, 2015.

"A family doesn't support some of their children better than the other children," she said. "They share the money, and this is what I wish colleges were doing. But it's not the way it's going. There are priority sports, and the priority means how much media attention does it get."[17]

TRANSGENDER ATHLETES

Sports groups, like society itself, are just beginning to recognize the concerns and interests of the transgender population. "We had more and more schools who said, 'We have a student who is transitioning or transitioned,'" explained Jamey Harrison, deputy director of the governing body of high school sports in Texas. "I think, without question, it has become much more of a common issue than it had previously been." Some athletic organizations, particularly the International Olympic Committee, have established very specific hormone-testing policies to determine eligibility, but high school coaches and athletic directors are coping with minors and small budgets. Essentially, high school leaders are making up their own rules, state by state. The Nebraska School Activities Association, for example, assembles a Gender Identity Eligibility committee composed of a physician, a psychiatrist, a school administrator and an association staff member to make definitive decisions on an athlete's gender placement.[18]

The issue is especially challenging because some people suspect that athletes who have transitioned from male to female might have a physical advantage over their peers, at least until their hormone therapy (which not every transgender person chooses to have) is complete. No one has reliable data yet on the number of transgender high school athletes (about 0.6 percent of the adult population identifies as transgender, according to federal data from 2016). The issue also raises significant emotional factors. Consider this comment from "Olivia," an athlete born male but now identifying as female: "Imagine you are practicing your favorite sport one day when somebody comes and tells you that you are not able to participate on the team. Not only does this take away your right to play, but it takes away something that defines you."[19]

Some schools choose to determine participation by the sex on a student's birth certificate, perhaps the most restrictive policy. Others allow participation as determined by the student's expressed gender. In such cases, the student must provide documentation including proof of at least a year of hormone therapy. But hormone therapy can be expensive and inconvenient, and thus not a choice for everyone. The fairest test, according to Texas Children's Hospital endocrinologist David Paul, is a student's testosterone level. But even then, there are no simple answers. "The problem is," Paul says, "what testosterone level confers an advantage?" Thus, there are no easy or inexpensive solutions on the horizon.[20]

If anything, the world of sports has been more accommodating to transgender athletes than the public, which may lag in its understanding of gender identity issues. If so, Renee Richards deserves much of the credit.

A Reluctant Pioneer

Richard Raskind was a successful eye surgeon, husband and father who had been captain of the men's tennis team at Yale. At age 40, all seemed well, but Raskind felt unfulfilled. "I had this other side of me that kept emerging and that kept pushing back, until finally it just wasn't possible to submerge Renee anymore and Renee won out."[21]

"Renee" was a woman who moved to California to start a new life after gender reassignment. She matters to all of us because in 1977 she became the first transgender woman to play in a professional tennis tournament. The tournament was the U.S. Open and it took place in Forest Hills, New York, just a short walk from Richard Raskind's childhood home.

Controversy raged over whether Richards should be allowed to compete as a woman. At 6 feet, 2 inches and with a powerful left-handed serve, she was a daunting opponent. "I never had any intention of playing in the U.S. Open," Richards said, "but when they said, 'You're not allowed to play,' that changed everything. I said, 'You can't tell me what I can or cannot do.'" When the Tennis Association went to court to challenge Renee's right to play, it hired top New York lawyers and brought in witness after witness. Richards' attorney had just one witness, but she was a former world No. 1 and a tennis icon: Billie Jean King.

"My lawyer had an affidavit from Billie Jean King that said she had met me," explained Richards, "that I was a woman, that I was entitled to play, and that I couldn't be denied. And that was it. We won."[22]

To this day, Raskind/Richards is the only player in history to reach the top level in both men's and women's competitions. She was a reluctant pioneer. "The whole world seemed to be looking for me to be their Joan of Arc," she said. Despite never having been an activist, Renee is now hailed for her courage. But her perspective is different: "I am first and last an individual."[23]

Taking the Lead

As we near the 50th anniversary of Title IX, we still struggle to find an equitable answer to the question of gender fairness. The tenacity of those who stood in the gymnasium doorway and blocked women from entering is sobering. Yet thanks to the pioneering efforts of individuals such as Renee Richards and a few gymnasts at Brown University, progress has been made. It is worth remembering that in 1971, as female athletes began demanding more opportunities at Brown, the women's athletic program was funded by bake sales and had a reserve account of $2,000.

CAN SPORTS BE TOO VIOLENT?

Many consider violence in sports a natural part of the game. But for almost everyone, there comes a moment when things cross a line. For example, "I've been coaching football for a long time," an older man said, "but I have never seen such a dangerous play. If that's allowed, it's not a sport."[24] The play the man was describing would not seem out of the ordinary to most fans. On the first play of the game, the quarterback rolled to his right and threw an incomplete pass. As his momentum carried him toward the sideline, a defensive player charged across the field, lowered his head and hit the quarterback in the small of his back. The player's head snapped back, and he soon left the game with injuries to his knee and back. The offending player was penalized for unnecessary roughness but stayed in the game.

What makes this play so remarkable is that it took place just outside Tokyo and matched two Japanese college teams, Nihon and Kwansei Gakuin. What is even more unusual is that the play created a viral sensation and precipitated a national conversation about the inherent dangers of the game and its place in Japanese society.

Perhaps we can use a Japanese lens for just a moment to consider violence in sport, a topic that has been frequently in the American news media ever since the discovery of chronic traumatic encephalopathy (CTE), a degenerative brain disorder associated with repetitive head trauma. Several studies have linked CTE to suicidal behavior, dementia and memory loss. Although professional athletes may be at highest risk for

NIGERIAN PATHOLOGIST DISCOVERS CTE

As a child in Nigeria, Dr. Bennet Omalu had little opportunity to follow American football — he didn't watch games, he didn't know the teams and he certainly didn't know the players. That changed in 2002 when, as a neuropathologist, he was assigned to do an autopsy on Mike Webster, one of the all-time great Pittsburgh Steelers' players. Omalu discovered a brain condition, chronic traumatic encephalopathy or CTE, that provided evidence of the dangers of playing football.

"In my opinion," said Omalu, "over 90 percent of players who play to the professional level have some degree of this disease." These players have been exposed to thousands of blows to the head over the course of their careers. But at first, when Omalu sent word of his research to the NFL, the organization did not even acknowledge his letter.

In time, of course, the dangers of CTE have been recognized by football coaches and administrators everywhere, but Omalu does not believe enough steps have been taken to safeguard players. "There are no rules that say we must play football the way it's played today. How we play football is not how we played 40 years ago."

Source: "How Nigerian Doctor Discovered Concussion Trauma in American Football Players," scitechafrica.com.

CTE, up to 3.8 million sports-related concussions occur in the United States each year at all levels; younger players are not immune.[25]

The football incident has shaken Japan, a country with a solemn commitment to "fair play" in sports, and has prompted coaches, university officials and politicians to question whether existing rules are adequate to quell the growing violence. The father of the injured quarterback, for example, filed a complaint with the police. The Japanese football association suspended the defensive player indefinitely and issued a warning to his coach. Other teams canceled their games with Nihon, turning the school into something of a pariah. The defensive player later said, "I don't think I have a right to continue playing football, and I have no intention to do so."[26]

Teddy Roosevelt's Summit

Would something like this reaction ever happen in the U.S.? Remarkably, it did, more than a century ago. The year was 1905 and although football was popular, it was becoming too brutal for many — 18 American boys died that year playing football, many from internal injuries, broken necks and concussions. The Washington Post reported that "nearly every death may be traced to 'unnecessary roughness.' Picked up unconscious from beneath a mass of other players, it was generally found that the victim had been kicked in the head or stomach, so as to cause internal injuries or concussion of the brain, which, sooner or later, ended life."[27]

President Teddy Roosevelt decided something needed to be done to save the game, especially as it promoted what he called the "strenuous life," a form of manliness he thought was needed to prepare the nation for tough times. "I believe in rough games and in rough, manly sports," Roosevelt explained. "I do not feel any particular sympathy for the person who gets battered about a good deal so long as it is not fatal."[28]

At the time football injuries were often caused by the style of play. The rules called for an extremely rough kind of game. A first down, for example, required just five yards, not 10, and the forward pass was illegal, so the game's basic strategy was to use a mass formation to creep just a few feet forward each play. As Nate Jackson, former NFL player and accomplished author, puts it, "Not much misdirection and no downfield action. Every play was shot from a cannon."[29]

To calm the general public, Roosevelt called a football summit at the White House, attended by coaches and athletic advisers from the powerhouses of college football: Harvard, Princeton and Yale. The charge he gave to the meeting was to "reduce the element of brutality in play." Roosevelt was no stranger to a rough lifestyle. A veteran of the Spanish-American War, and a former commissioner of the New York Police Department, his own personal life led him to a belief that Americans should be a nation of scrappy fighters — and football was just the game to teach them how to do it.

Fortunately, for the future of football, the summit created several rule changes that had a transformative effect on the game. The new rules spread action across the field and dramatically reduced the likelihood of fatalities. First, the forward pass was legalized, then mass formations were abolished and the first-down distance was doubled from five yards to 10. A neutral zone was established between offense and defense. Officials were instructed to stop the game when a player fell on the ball in order to avoid heaps of men leaping on top of each other, and players could now kick the ball down the field. Some observers were critical (one cartoonist drew football players in tutus), but there was improvement. In 1906, the year after the summit, 11 players were killed, the same as in 1907.[30]

These rule changes led to a safer game, but they also made for a better and more exciting one. In 1913 Notre Dame became famous for its use of the forward pass, and in 1920 the National Football League was formed. But people sometimes drag their feet when it comes to changing a game they love. The most important safety feature — the helmet — would not be mandated until much later, in 1939. When sports organizations are not open to changing the rules, other remedies must be sought. In the case of hockey, for example, fighting is part of the game that fans have come to expect, even celebrate — "A puck is a hard rubber disc that hockey players strike when they can't hit one another" — but even fighting that is tolerated or encouraged can go too far.[31]

WATCH THAT STICK!

Boston Bruins hockey coach Milt Schmidt had seen enough. He purchased two dozen helmets and passed them out to his players. When he showed up for practice the next day, no one was wearing a helmet. He ordered the team to put on their helmets or get off the ice. When the team's star and one of hockey's all-time greats, Bobby Orr, slowly skated to the edge of the rink, the coach knew his plan was not going to work.[32]

What caused Coach Schmidt to ask players to wear helmets was a horrific stick-swinging battle between Boston's Ted Green and rookie Wayne Maki from the St. Louis Blues in an exhibition game played in Ottawa, Canada, on Sept. 21, 1969. During the exchange, Green happened to turn away just when Maki swung his stick, catching Green on his unprotected head. Green collapsed and was rushed to the hospital where five hours of surgery were required to stop his brain hemorrhaging and save his life.

The event was only a bit worse than most hockey fights, but it was enough for the media to pressure Canadian authorities to act. The Ottawa police investigated the case and two months later swore out criminal charges against both players for "assault occasioning bodily harm." A few months later, both players were acquitted of charges and each eventually returned to the ice.[33]

Surprisingly, nothing in hockey changed. Bob Gainey, the general manager of the Montreal Canadiens, said that adding rules to stop fighting would diminish the "robust physical play that attracts all of us to the game." This early attempt to make hockey safer through the court system had failed.[34]

CHANGE IS HARD

The Maki-Green confrontation marked the first time in the history of professional sports that police became involved with player conduct because of something that happened during a game. But the fact that Maki and Green were each acquitted may have slowed the progress of reform. It took until March 2010 for the NHL to finally vote to ban blind-side hits to the head. Meanwhile, in basketball the NBA owners gave the commissioner the power to fine and suspend players who fought, and commissioners have not been reluctant to use that power.[35]

In the early days of sports, leagues made an effort to ensure that any conflicts were resolved in-house. But as sports have evolved in terms of fan scrutiny and sophistication, we have learned that the law, through its instrument — the courts — can play a role in stemming unnecessary violence.

UPON FURTHER REVIEW

1. Imagine that you have been appointed federal judge in the Jenkins case. What would your ruling be?

2. Should athletes be subjected to testosterone or other hormone-level tests to determine whether they can participate in sports events? What are the alternatives that might be better?

3. If football were invented today, would the rules be different? What, if any, rules in football or hockey would you change to protect the health of the players?

NOTES

1. Katherine Q. Seelye and Daniel Victor, "Yawkey Way, Where Red Sox Fans Converge, Will Be Renamed Over Racism Concerns," New York Times, April 26, 2018.

2. James Wellman and Walter B. Peet, "The Story of the Harvard-Yale Race 1852-1912" (New York: Harper and Brothers, 1962), 15.

3. Sam Richmond, "College football history: Here's when the 1st game was played," NCAA .com, Nov. 6, 2017.

4. Roger I. Abrams, "Sports Justice: The Law & the Business of Sports" (Lebanon, NH: University Press of New England, 2010), 69.

5. Richard Johnson, "Here's why Mark Emmert's comment on the NCAA embracing the Olympic model of compensation is meaningless," SBNation.com, Mar. 3, 2018.

6. Abrams, "Sports Justice," 75.

7. Jeff Borzello, Jonathan Givony and Myron Metcalf, "Tough talk on corruption, one-and-done, but commission misses the mark," ESPN.com, Apr. 25, 2018.

8. Marc Tracy, "Investigation? N.C.A.A. Scrutiny? Business as Usual in Grassroots Hoops," New York Times, May 21, 2018.

9. Michael McCann, "NCAA Amateurism to Go Back Under Courtroom Spotlight in Jenkins Trial," si.com, Apr. 2, 2018.

10. Abrams, "Sports Justice," 103.

11. Adrian Kajumba, "Winning the Wimbledon women's final really is Garbine Muguruza's cup of tea," mirror.co.uk., July 16, 2017.

12. Bill Littlefield, "Brown University: Revisiting the Case for Title IX," wbur.org, June 23, 2012.

13. Adele Jackson-Gibson, "Title IX's 45th Anniversary: Four Title IX lawsuits that rocked the world of women's sports," excellesports.com, June 23, 2017.

14. Littlefield, "Brown University."

15. Jackson-Gibson, "Title IX's 45th Anniversary."

16. Kay More, "ESPNW Summit: Title IX and 40 Years of Improving Sports. And Education," www.wired.com, Oct.25, 2012.

17. Littlefield, "Brown University."

18. Nebraska School Activities Association—Gender Participation Policy, NSAA-statc. s3.amazonaws.com.

19. Malika Andrews, "How Should High Schools Define Sexes for Transgender Athletes?" New York Times, Nov. 8, 2017.

20. Ibid.

21. Steve Tignor, "40 years later, Renee Richards' breakthrough is as important as ever," www.tennis.com, Sept. 20, 2017.

22. Ibid.

23. Ibid.

24. Ken Belson, "The Football Hit Felt All Over Japan," New York Times, May 22, 2018.

25. Ann McKee et al., "Chronic Traumatic Encephalopathy in Athletes: Progressive Tauopathy following Repetitive Head Injury," www.ncbi.nlm.nih.gov.

26. Belson, "The Football Hit."

27. Katie Zezima, "How Teddy Roosevelt Helped Save Football," Washington Post, May 29, 2014.

28. Christopher Klein, "How Teddy Roosevelt Saved Football," www.history.com, Sept. 6, 2012.

29. Nate Jackson, "What If Football Were Reinvented Today?" in Mike Pesca, "Upon Further Review" (New York: Hachette Book Group, 2018), 105.

30. "Did Theodore Roosevelt Really Save Football?" DailyHistory.org.

31. Mark Stoltz, "Top 10 Hockey Quotes," bleacherreport.com, Sept. 19, 2008.

32. Brian McFarlane, "A Dreadful Incident: Green Versus Maki," ithappenedinhockey.com, 2011.

33. Ibid.

34. Roger I. Abrams, "A Dubious Anniversary," Huffington Post, Nov. 19, 2009.

35. David DuPree, "NBA Plans Stiff Fines for Fights," Washington Post, Mar. 2, 1977.

Appendix A
AP Sports Guidelines and Style

Football:

The spellings of some frequently used words and phrases:

blitz (n., v.)	out-of-bounds (adj.)
cornerback	pick six (n.)
end line	pick-six (adj)
end zone	pitchout (n.)
fair catch	place kick
fourth-and-1 (adj.)	place-kicker
fullback	play off (v.)
goal line	playoff (n., adj.)
goal-line stand	quarterback
halfback	runback (n.)
handoff	running back
kick off (v.)	split end
kickoff (n., adj.)	tailback
left guard	tight end
linebacker	touchback
lineman	touchdown
line of scrimmage	wideout
nickel back	wide receiver
onside kick	X's and O's
out of bounds (adv.)	

Numbers:

Use figures for yardage: The 5-yard line, the 10-yard line, a 5-yard pass play, he plunged in from the 2, he ran 6 yards, a 7-yard gain; a fourth-and-2 play.

Some other uses of numbers: The final score was 21-14. The team won its fourth game in 10 starts. The team record is 4-5-1.

Playoffs:
wild-card round, wild card, divisional round, NFC championship game, AFC championship game.

Super Bowl:
Refer to the Super Bowl by the year of the game, not by Roman numeral. If a counter is needed, use cardinal numbers: 2017 Super Bowl preferred over Super Bowl 51; do not use Super Bowl LI.

    League: National Football League, or NFL.

    TD: Acceptable in all references to touchdown.

    O-line, D-line: Acceptable abbreviations for offensive line, defensive line.

    Statistics:

All football games, whether using the 1- or 2-point conversion, use the same summary style.

The visiting team always is listed first.

Field goals are measured from the point where the ball was kicked — not the line of scrimmage. The goal posts are 10 yards behind the goal lines. Include that distance.

Abbreviate team names to four letters or fewer on the scoring and statistical lines as illustrated.

Use figures for par listings: He had a par 5 to finish 2-up for the round, a par-4 hole; a 7-under-par 64, the par-3 seventh hole.

The passing line shows, in order: completions-attempts-interceptions.

A Sample Agate Package:

Jets-Giants Stats:

N.Y. Jets	7	10	7	0_24	
N.Y. Giants	0	7	14	14	14_35

First Quarter
NYJ_Rhodes 11 fumble return (Nugent kick), 8:36.

Second Quarter
NYG_Ward 8 run (Tynes kick), 10:54.
NYJ_B.Smith 16 pass from Pennington (Nugent kick), :33.
NYJ_FG Nugent 47, :00.

Third Quarter
NYG_Jacobs 19 run (Tynes kick), 11:17.
NYJ_L.Washington 98 kickoff return (Nugent kick), 11:03.
NYG_Shockey 13 pass from Manning (Tynes kick), :33.

Fourth Quarter
NYG_Burress 53 pass from Manning (Tynes kick), 7:52.
NYG_Ross 43 interception return (Tynes kick), 3:15.
A_78,809.

	NYJ	NYG
First Downs	16	21
Total Net Yards	277	374
Rushes-Yards	22-55	39-188
Passing	222	186
Punt Returns	2-20	2-16
Kickoff Returns	5-200	3-62
Interceptions Ret.	1-1	3-68
Comp-Att-Int	21-36-3	13-25-1
Sacked-Yards Lost	1-7	0-0
Punts	4-45.3	5-46.8
Fumbles-Lost	0-0	1-1
Penalties-Yards	6-40	3-37
Time of Possession	26:15	33:45

Individual Statistics:

RUSHING_N.Y. Jets, T.Jones 13-36, L.Washington 9-13, Pennington 2-6, B.Smith 1-0. N.Y. Giants, Jacobs 20-100, Ward 13-56, Manning 4-17, Droughns 2-15.

PASSING_N.Y. Jets, Pennington 21-36-3-229. N.Y. Giants, Manning 13-25-1-186.

RECEIVING_N.Y. Jets, Coles 8-89, Cotchery 4-31, Baker 3-52, B.Smith 3-44, T.Jones 2-14, L.Washington 1-(minus 1). N.Y. Giants, Burress 5-124, Ward 3-8, Shockey 2-33, Moss 1-10, Matthews 1-6, Hedgecock 1-5.

MISSED FIELD GOAL_N.Y. Jets, Nugent 42 (WL).

The rushing and receiving paragraph for individual leaders shows attempts and yardage gained. The passing paragraph shows completions, attempts, interceptions and total yards gained.

Standings:
The form for **professional standings:**

American Conference

East

	W	L	T	Pct.	PF	PA
y-New England	12	3	0	.800	464	321
N.Y. Jets	8	7	0	.533	360	344
Buffalo	6	9	0	.400	351	385
y-clinched division						

The form for college **conference standings:**

	Conference				All Games			
	W	L	PF	PA	W	L	PF	PA
West Virginia	5	2	240	126	11	2	515	235

In college conference standings, limit team names to nine letters or fewer. Abbreviate as necessary.

All-America, All-American:
The Associated Press recognizes only one All-America football and basketball team each year. In football, only Walter Camp's selections through 1924, and the AP selections after that, are recognized. Do not call anyone not listed on either the Camp or AP roster an All-America selection.

Similarly, do not call anyone who was not an AP selection an All-America basketball player.

The first All-America men's basketball team was chosen in 1948.

Use All-American when referring specifically to an individual:

All-American Breanna Stewart, or She is an All-American.

Use All-America when referring to the team:

All-America team, or All-America selection.

Athletic Director:
Use the singular athletic unless otherwise in a formal title.

Titles:
Capitalize or use lowercase according to guidelines in AP Stylebook's main section. Job descriptions, field positions and informal titles are lowercase: coach John Calipari; for-

ward Alex Morgan; general manager John Elway. Some other informal titles commonly used in sports include general manager, trainer, team doctor, manager, captain.

Collective Nouns:
Nouns that denote a unit take singular verbs and pronouns: class, committee, crowd, family, group, herd, jury, orchestra, team.

Some usage examples: The committee is meeting to set its agenda. The jury reached its verdict. A herd of cattle was sold.

Team names and musical group names that are plural take plural verbs. The Yankees are in first place. The Jonas Brothers are popular.

Team or group names with no plural forms also take plural verbs: The Miami Heat are battling for third place. Other examples: Orlando Magic, Oklahoma City Thunder, Utah Jazz, Alabama Crimson Tide.

Most singular names take singular verbs, including places and university names in sports: Coldplay is on tour. Boston is favored in the playoffs. Stanford is in the NCAA Tournament.

Some proper names that are plural in form take a singular verb: Brooks Brothers is holding a sale.

Plural in Form:
Some words that are plural in form become collective nouns and take singular verbs when the group or quantity is regarded as a unit.

Right: A thousand bushels is a good yield. (A unit.)

Right: A thousand bushels were created. (Individual items.)

Right: The data is sound. (A unit.)

Right: The data have been carefully collected. (Individual items.)

Yard Lines:
Use figures to indicate the dividing lines on a football field and distance traveled: 40-yard line, he plunged in from the 2, he ran 6 yards, a 7-yard gain.

Scores:
Use figures exclusively, placing a hyphen between the totals of the winning and losing teams: The Reds defeated the Red Sox 4-3, the Giants scored a 12-6 football victory over the Cardinals, the golfer had a 5 on the first hole but finished with a 2-under-par score.

Use a comma in this format: Boston 6, Baltimore 5.

See individual listings for each sport for further details.

Fractions:
In general, follow the **fractions** entry in the Stylebook's main section, writing fractions with two numerals separated by a forward slash: ½, ⅔ or ¾. Do not use single

fractional characters, which do not appear properly for some computer systems. For mixed numbers, separate the whole integer from the fraction with a space: J.J. Watt had 2 ½ sacks, Matt Cain pitched 7 ⅔ innings. In baseball, avoid using fractions to describe outings of less than an inning. Simply write: Craig Kimbrel got the last two outs for the save.

Exceptions: Spellings for some frequently used words are exceptions to Webster's New World College Dictionary, made for consistency in handling sports stories.

backboard	**backstretch**
backcourt	**backstroke**
backfield	**ballclub**
backhand	**ballgame**
backspin	**ballpark**
backstop	**ballplayer**

THE ASSOCIATED PRESS STYLEBOOK

The Associated Press Stylebook provides fundamental guidelines for spelling, language, punctuation, usage and journalistic style. A new edition is published each year, while the AP Stylebook Online is updated throughout the year. The preceding examples were excerpted from the 2018 AP Stylebook's sports chapter.

While many writers and editors are most familiar with the printed AP Stylebook, AP also offers an e-book edition and the digital AP Stylebook Online, both searchable and portable so users can have style guidance handy when covering sporting events.

— Colleen Newvine, Product Manager, AP Stylebook

Appendix B

CODE *of* ETHICS

PREAMBLE

Members of the Society of Professional Journalists believe that public enlightenment is the forerunner of justice and the foundation of democracy. Ethical journalism strives to ensure the free exchange of information that is accurate, fair and thorough. An ethical journalist acts with integrity. The Society declares these four principles as the foundation of ethical journalism and encourages their use in its practice by all people in all media.

SEEK TRUTH AND REPORT IT

Ethical journalism should be accurate and fair. Journalists should be honest and courageous in gathering, reporting and interpreting information.

Journalists should:

- Take responsibility for the accuracy of their work. Verify information before releasing it. Use original sources whenever possible.
- Remember that neither speed nor format excuses inaccuracy.
- Provide context. Take special care not to misrepresent or oversimplify in promoting, previewing or summarizing a story.
- Gather, update and correct information throughout the life of a news story.
- Be cautious when making promises, but keep the promises they make.
- Identify sources clearly. The public is entitled to as much information as possible to judge the reliability and motivations of sources.
- Consider sources' motives before promising anonymity. Reserve anonymity for sources who may face danger, retribution or other harm, and have information that cannot be obtained elsewhere. Explain why anonymity was granted.

- Diligently seek subjects of news coverage to allow them to respond to criticism or allegations of wrongdoing.
- Avoid undercover or other surreptitious methods of gathering information unless traditional, open methods will not yield information vital to the public.
- Be vigilant and courageous about holding those with power accountable. Give voice to the voiceless.
- Support the open and civil exchange of views, even views they find repugnant.
- Recognize a special obligation to serve as watchdogs over public affairs and government. Seek to ensure that the public's business is conducted in the open, and that public records are open to all.
- Provide access to source material when it is relevant and appropriate.
- Boldly tell the story of the diversity and magnitude of the human experience. Seek sources whose voices we seldom hear.
- Avoid stereotyping. Journalists should examine the ways their values and experiences may shape their reporting.
- Label advocacy and commentary.
- Never deliberately distort facts or context, including visual information. Clearly label illustrations and re-enactments.
- Never plagiarize. Always attribute.

MINIMIZE HARM

Ethical journalism treats sources, subjects, colleagues and members of the public as human beings deserving of respect.

Journalists should:

- Balance the public's need for information against potential harm or discomfort.
- Pursuit of the news is not a license for arrogance or undue intrusiveness.
- Show compassion for those who may be affected by news coverage. Use heightened sensitivity when dealing with juveniles, victims of sex crimes, and sources or subjects who are inexperienced or unable to give consent. Consider cultural differences in approach and treatment.
- Recognize that legal access to information differs from an ethical justification to publish or broadcast.
- Realize that private people have a greater right to control information about themselves than public figures and others who seek power, influence or attention. Weigh the consequences of publishing or broadcasting personal information.
- Avoid pandering to lurid curiosity, even if others do.
- Balance a suspect's right to a fair trial with the public's right to know. Consider the implications of identifying criminal suspects before they face legal charges.

- Consider the long-term implications of the extended reach and permanence of publication. Provide updated and more complete information as appropriate.

ACT INDEPENDENTLY

The highest and primary obligation of ethical journalism is to serve the public.

Journalists should:

- Avoid conflicts of interest, real or perceived. Disclose unavoidable conflicts.
- Refuse gifts, favors, fees, free travel and special treatment, and avoid political and other outside activities that may compromise integrity or impartiality, or may damage credibility.
- Be wary of sources offering information for favors or money; do not pay for access to news. Identify content provided by outside sources, whether paid or not.
- Deny favored treatment to advertisers, donors or any other special interests, and resist internal and external pressure to influence coverage.
- Distinguish news from advertising and shun hybrids that blur the lines between the two. Prominently label sponsored content.

BE ACCOUNTABLE AND TRANSPARENT

Ethical journalism means taking responsibility for one's work and explaining one's decisions to the public.

Journalists should:

- Explain ethical choices and processes to audiences. Encourage a civil dialogue with the public about journalistic practices, coverage and news content.
- Respond quickly to questions about accuracy, clarity and fairness.
- Acknowledge mistakes and correct them promptly and prominently. Explain corrections and clarifications carefully and clearly.
- Expose unethical conduct in journalism, including within their organizations.
- Abide by the same high standards they expect of others.

The SPJ Code of Ethics is a statement of abiding principles supported by additional explanations and position papers [at spj.org] that address changing journalistic practices. It is not a set of rules, rather a guide that encourages all who engage in journalism to take responsibility for the information they provide, regardless of medium. The code should be read as a whole; individual principles should not be taken out of context. It is not, nor can it be under the First Amendment, legally enforceable.

Appendix C
Glossary of News and Sports Terms

Actuality: Recorded voice or natural (nat) sound from a news event inserted in a broadcast story; includes quotes from coaches and players, sounds of band, crowd cheering.

Advance: A story about an upcoming game that compares teams and players, discusses team records and gives lineups.

Allusion: A reference to a well-known person, place or event, often literary or historical, in relation to a current person or topic. Grantland Rice used an allusion to the Four Horsemen, known in dramatic lore as Famine, Pestilence, Destruction and Death, to describe four backs who played for Notre Dame in 1924-26.

Anonymous sources: Unnamed sources, known only to reporters and their supervisors, who become primary sources, usually in a breaking news story.

Associated Press: Largest wire service in United States; delivers global news to member media continuously.

Associated Press Stylebook: Style guide published by the Associated Press; regarded as the standard for print and online writing.

Attribution: Crediting a quotation or information to a source.

Attributive: Type of verb connecting quotation or paraphrase with the verb's subject (source); "said" is the preferred attributive verb.

Backgrounder: A document or story that contains information about the sport, team, coaches, events and issues that could potentially be covered in future stories.

Batting average: The classic measure of batting proficiency. Ted Williams once had a batting average above .400. Calculated as base hits divided by at-bats, not counting walks, hit by pitchers or sacrifices.

B-copy: Body paragraphs, usually background material, written before an event ends if it will end too close to deadline to allow time for writing the entire story.

Beat reporter: A reporter who covers the same team or the same sport on a regular basis.

Behind-the-scenes sources: People who provide pertinent information or ideas for stories but aren't necessarily used as primary or secondary sources in the actual story.

Biography: A person's life story; in this context, highlighted specifically by key sports accomplishments.

Blog: An online journal maintained by a person or entity to engage a community in conversation; often themed, blogs invite web users' participation; allow bloggers to add entries 24/7.

Blurb: A summary sentence, sometimes the nut graf of the story, inserted between the headline and the text of an online news story; gives reader concise information in fewer words. A short promo on a book cover.

Boilerplate: Final paragraph of news release, provides basic information about the organization or program sponsoring the news release; same paragraph included on all releases from that sponsor; historically, type that was set in a tray, one lead letter at a time, and saved for repeated use.

Box score: A statistical tabulation of a game giving the names and positions of the players and a record of their individual performances; first appeared in a newspaper in 1913.

B-roll: Video or visuals without audio; generic footage of place or event; used to give setting, background visuals for story.

Byline: Name of reporter, usually at top of print story and beginning and end of broadcast story on location.

Caption: Words describing the action and identifying the people in a photo; usually written by photographer; also called "cutline."

Circular story structure: Story organization in which the end circles back to make a connection with the lead; usually used in feature stories, profiles.

Cliché: Old saying, overused phrase; avoid in all stories.

Closed-ended questions: Questions that limit sources in how they're able to respond. Also called yes-no questions.

Code of ethics: Written statement of expectations or conduct in the pursuit of a profession or within a workplace; see Society of Professional Journalists' Code of Ethics in appendix B.

Column: Regular opinion feature by one author; identified by column head.

Column head: Indicates material is an opinion column or review containing personal commentary; column head includes tagline (column name), byline and mug shot of columnist.

Commercial use: Use of copyrighted material in a way that will make a profit for a person or business; is illegal without written permission; applies to team logos or mascots depicted in advertising paid for by someone other than the owner of the trademark or copyright.

Copyright: Legal protection of the right to ownership of an original work produced in a tangible form (writing, photos, art, etc.); protects works from use by others without permission.

Cutline: Traditional term for words describing the action and identifying the people in a photo; usually written by photographer; also called "caption."

Dateline: Appears at beginning of a story or news release; indicates where story originated if it is not written locally; historically, dateline included the date the story was written.

Delayed lead: Story lead in which the focus is not known for several paragraphs; also called indirect lead.

Diction: Style of speaking based on your choice of words, formal or informal, such as "The thing that really gets me about that guy" versus "What most disturbs me about Professor Snooze"; also, enunciation or style of delivery.

Direct lead: Story lead that tells most of the 5 Ws and an H in the first one or two paragraphs.

Direct quotation: An exact, word-for-word account of what a person said, enclosed in quotation marks and attributed to the source.

Down style: Headline with only the first word and proper nouns capitalized; also called "sentence style."

Embargo: On a news release or wire story, request by source that media not publish the story until a specified date.

End mark: Symbol indicating the end of a page or story in hard or electronic copy; standard end marks include — ### —, — 30 —, — end —, — more —.

Euphemism: A word used in place of another to make the topic sound less harsh; dressing up plain language; AP style is to use literal, factually correct words, not euphemisms.

Fact sheet: A list of facts; similar to a news release in that it is a way to communicate information quickly and easily to the media.

Fair comment: Legal protection for journalists who offer opinion or commentary on the performance of anyone in the public eye; comments must be based on correct, factual information and not be intentionally malicious.

Feature: Story that focuses on people, places, issues or the human interest side of story; less timely, can run anytime and be equally newsworthy; if feature has a news hook, should run within a few days of news event.

Flash interview: An unusually quick and informal interview when a reporter and athlete or coach speak just outside the locker room or off the field.

Follow-up question: Question asked to clarify or expand on an original question.

Gamer: Full story, usually with quotations, about a game or competition.

Gender-biased language: Language that favors one gender over another; for example, avoid use of language that assumes all sports fans are 20-something males or that a female reporter is less capable of covering sports than her male counterparts.

Gutter: Narrow strip of white space between columns of text; especially center of double truck.

Hard copy: Story in print; script for news or sportscaster.

Headline: Summarizes the story; is written by copy editors; appears in larger type above the story it describes.

Homer: Reporter who shows bias for the team he or she primarily covers.

Hot take: A strong opinion likely written for the purpose of promoting a reaction.

Idiom: A collection of terms and phrases used and understood by people who are familiar with the literal as well as the idiomatic meanings of words, e.g., "sacked" as a verb means to put things, usually groceries, into a sack, but in football "sacked" means that the quarterback was tackled behind the line before he could pass the ball.

Inverted pyramid: Most common structure for news stories; information is organized in most important to least important order.

-isms: Short for words that end in -ism, such as ageism, racism, sexism; a practice likely to offend large segments of audience.

Lead: Beginning of news story, introduces topic; may be the first sentence or several paragraphs; also called an intro.

Leading questions: Questions that try to lead the source to respond in a certain manner.

Libel: A false written statement that damages a person's character and causes that person to be ridiculed or shunned, or jeopardizes his or her occupational credibility.

Line score: A summary of a game's score displayed in the form of a horizontal table; for example, in baseball as an inning-by-inning record of the runs scored followed by the total of each team's runs, hits and errors.

Link: A connection between pages within a website and other pages or sites; a shortcut to reach supplementary material.

Live coverage: Broadcast coverage of an event in progress, such as a game, awards ceremony or halftime show.

Local angle: Focus of a news story on a local person, place or issue within a larger story to increase story appeal to local audience.

Material sources: Physical items such as record books, media guides or other stories that can provide information for a reporter.

Media credentials: Passes assigned to individual reporters or news organizations that provide access to games, news conferences, practices or other game-related activities.

Minutiae: Precise details or small, trifling matters, depending on your point of view.

Model T: MSNBC's name for an organization pattern of online news stories; 5 Ws form the horizontal top of the T, chunks of information in descending order of importance form the trunk.

Mug shot: Head and shoulders photo; close-up photo of a person's face, usually run 1 to 2 inches with a story or column; may be of writer, source or subject of story.

Nat sound: Natural sound of an environment such as a game; used as sound bites to capture flavor, ambience of event.

News conference: A formal interview setting designed for sources to share information simultaneously with members of the media and, usually, for the media to ask questions. In sports, the source may be an athlete, official or coach speaking to an audience of mostly sports reporters. Also see "press conference."

News release: Publicity tool; information sent to media with the intention of attracting media interest that will result in a story about a topic or source.

Nut graf: Paragraph or point in a story where the reader or listener knows exactly what the story is about; may be first paragraph or may occur several paragraphs into the story.

Open-ended questions: Questions that ask an opinion or interpretation from a source.

Paraphrase: A summary of what a source said, attributed to that source, without changing the meaning; does not require quotation marks.

Participatory journalism: When a reporter becomes a participant in the story he or she is covering; in another sense, this also happens when citizens contribute their own blogs, photos or videos to a mainstream journalism outlet.

Podcasting: One way of broadcasting via the internet; audio and/or video packaged together in a "pod," made available in RSS format to users of iPods and devices with similar retrieval software.

Post: To upload information, story to website.

Postgame analysis: An attempt to break down the various successes and failures of a team during a recent game.

Press box: A group of seats at an athletic event that usually provide a good view of the entire field, reserved and equipped for members of the media.

Press conference: Prefer more inclusive term: "news conference."

Press row: A row of seats at an athletic event that are reserved for the press, sometimes at courtside.

Primary sources: Sources with information or opinions vital to the outcome of a story.

Private person: In law, a person unintentionally exposed to public view who suffers mental distress as a result of the publicity; protected from invasion of privacy.

Privilege: A defense against libel; journalists' right to report what government officials say and do in the conduct of their official duties without fear of being sued for libel.

Pronouncer: Phonetic spelling inserted in parentheses [pah-REN-tha-sees] for unfamiliar names and words in a broadcast script.

Public figure: Person who voluntarily seeks a role of prominence in society or who gains persuasive power and influence through that role or who intentionally inserts himself or herself into public controversies; includes professional athletes, coaches.

Quotation: Citation and attribution of the exact words of a source.

Quote sheet: A written transcript of a news conference.

Recap: A brief summary, one to three paragraphs, on the outcome of a game or competition.

Scoop: Report a news story before competing media outlets do.

Scorekeeper: Someone who keeps score during a game and is responsible for compiling the official results.

Scrum: A small to medium-sized group of reporters, normally in a hallway or locker room, surrounding one source for media interviews.

Secondary headline: Sentence or phrases inserted between the main headline and the story; works with headline to add information and entice reader into the story; also called subhead or deck.

Secondary sources: Sources that aren't essential to the outcome of a story, but add information that makes a story more complete.

Sentence style: Headline with only the first word and proper nouns capitalized; also called "down style."

Shooting percentage: A measure of a basketball player's accuracy determined by dividing the number of attempts by the number of field goals made.

Sidebars: Short, related stories run in conjunction with a larger news story.

Slander: Spoken defamation of character; recorded words are considered libel, as are scripted words read during a broadcast, because they are in a tangible form.

Slug: Short label that identifies a story in process.

Sound bite: Prerecorded excerpt inserted in audio or video programming.

Source: People or reference material from which information is gathered for news stories.

Sports feature: Story about a person or issue related to sports; a player profile, a seasonal story about training camp or bowl selections, an informative, timeless story on, for example, sports medicine or nutrition.

Sports information director: Also known as media relations director, the person(s)responsible for managing information communications between teams and media; job includes preparing news releases, arranging news conferences and interviews, publishing a media guide and providing statistics and data to media during games; generally known as an SID.

Sports record book: Similar to an almanac, this compilation of top sports performances over time can be a valuable resource for writers; entries often include career leaders, longest plays, single bests and individual and team records; the book is typically updated at the end of each season.

Statistics: The collection, classification, analysis and interpretation of numerical facts that help sports writers analyze a game; commonly known as stats.

Streaming: Sending compressed audio and/or video in a continuous stream over the internet to be viewed as it arrives; programming from radio or television distributed via the internet; moving visual images delivered online.

Title IX: Now known as the Patsy Mink Equal Opportunity in Education Act (1972), this law essentially banned discrimination on the basis of sex; although the law itself doesn't mention sports, its passage led to the establishment of varsity athletic teams for women at the high school and collegiate levels.

Trademark: Name and/or logo registered by an entity such as a college or a business; users must have permission, and sometimes pay a fee, to reproduce a trademark in any context.

Troll: Social media users, specifically on Twitter, who simply send negative tweets to garner a reaction from the original person who tweeted.

Verification: Rechecking information for accuracy and validity.

Wire services: Membership organizations that gather news from around the world and distribute it to local members; the way most local media outlets receive national and international news.

Work made-for-hire: Work created for an employer, such as stories a reporter writes for a newspaper or website; the property of the employer, not the creator.

Wrap: A broadcast story that begins and ends with the reporter's voice "wrapped around" one or more actualities; also called a package.

Index